Contents

The Basics

Basic needs

To survive, everyone needs food, clothing and shelter. An average adult male must get at least 2000 calories a day to survive. Clothing protects us from the elements. We also need somewhere safe to live.

Many of us enjoy all of these. Many do not. The United Nations states that 800 million people starve every day. Somewhere on our planet, a child dies every few minutes – of hunger.

Fig 1.1 People still die of starvation

Other needs

As well as the basics, humans need other things to live a full life:

- clean water

- some form of education system

- a social infrastructure (e.g. good transport system, health care, police forces)

- justice and fairness.

DISCUSSION POINT

Do you think of yourself as rich or poor?

Fig 1.2 The North-South divide

A fair world?

A line can be drawn on a world map. Above the line (in the North or the developed world) most people have what they need and also much that they want. Below the line (in the South or the developing world) many people don't even have the basics. It has been claimed that the 10% of the world's population living in the North controls 90% of the world's wealth. In the North, obesity is a major problem; in the South, starvation. Both cause similar health problems.

100 million people in the world today are completely homeless. The World Bank says that 1.3 billion people live in absolute poverty. Such people often live on incomes equal to less than 50p a day. 30 million people every year die of hunger. A child in a developing country will have an illness every three weeks on average. The richest fifth of the world's population consume 45% of all meat and fish; the poorest fifth consume 5%.

Absolute poverty is when your life is threatened by how poor you are. Relative poverty just means that you are poor in relation to others in your society. Most of the world's absolute poverty is in the South.

DISCUSSION POINT

Is it right for a British family to spend thousands of pounds on a summer holiday when people on Earth are starving?

4

World Issues

Religion and Morality

Jim Green • Joe Walker

Hodder & Stoughton

A MEMBER OF THE HODDER HEADLINE GROUP

Joe Walker would like to thank Lorna and David for their patience yet again.

Also, thanks to Nikki Summers and Ross Brain for reading and commenting upon early drafts.

Jim Green would like to thank Bro. Daniel Faivre for his help and permission to draw on his book, *Transcendence, Prayer of People of Faith*.

Acknowledgements

The publishers would like to thank the following individuals, institutions and companies for permission to reproduce copyright illustrations in this book:

Andrew Ward/Life File, pages 5 top, 64 top; © Annie Griffiths Belt/CORBIS, page 46; AP by Greg Marinovich, page 24; Associated Press, pages 41 top left, 48 right, 54, 55, 58; Associated Press AP, pages 5 bottom, 6, 12, 29 left, 29 right, 33 bottom, 42, 43, 47, 49 left, 49 top right, 65 top left; Associated Press Department of Defense, page 53 bottom right; Associated Press Photo, page 30; Associated Press POOL, page 37 right; Atlantic Syndication Partners, page 16 left; Ben Buxton/Anti-Slavery International, page 16 left; © Bettmann/CORBIS, page 60 top left; Christine Osborne Pictures, page 57 bottom right; © Colin Garratt; Milepost 92 ½/CORBIS, page 13 right; © Dave G. Houser/CORBIS, page 50; © David Turnley/CORBIS, pages 44 left, 45 right; © Farrell Grehan/CORBIS, pages 62, 65 bottom left; Geoff Tompkinson/Science Photo Library, page 69 left; Hulton Archive, page 53 left; © Hulton Archive, pages 40 right, 53 top right; © IWM (Imperial War Museum), page 48 left; © Jennie Woodcock, Reflections Photolibrary/CORBIS, page 61 centre right; Jeremy Hoare/Life File, pages 60 top right, 65 bottom right; John Maier/Still Pictures, page 17; © Jorgen Schytte/Still Pictures, page 61 top left; © Kelly-Mooney Photography/CORBIS, pages 13 left, 33 left; Larry Bray/Telegraph Colour Library, pages 61 top right; PA News, page 69 right; PA News Photo Library, page 64 bottom; PA Photos, pages 8 left, 21, 25 left, 25 right; PA Photos/EPA, pages 4 left, 37 left, 52 right, 68; © Peter Johnson/CORBIS, pages 60 bottom left, 63; © Peter Turnley/CORBIS, pages 44 right, 45 left; © Philip Gould/CORBIS, page 57 bottom left; *Napoléon 1er sur le champ de bataille d'Eylau* by Baron Antoine-Jean Gros (9 février 1807), Photo RMN – Daniel Arnaudet, page 40 left; Popperfoto, page 32; R. Chapple/Telegraph Colour Library, page 61 bottom left; © Reuters NewMedia Inc./CORBIS, page 41 bottom left; © Richard Greenhill, page 61 bottom right; Richard Powers/Life File, pages 9, 16 top; © Sally A. Morgan, Ecoscene/CORBIS, page 52 left; © Sergio Dorantes/CORBIS, page 36; The Ronald Grant Archive, page 28; Tim Fisher/Life File, page 56; 20th Century Fox Film Company/The Ronald Grant Archive, page 8 right; Ulrike Preuss/Format Photographers, page 20; Westminster Interfaith (this group organises such pilgrimages), page 59.

The publishers would also like to thank the following for permission to reproduce material in this book: CAFOD for the extract from CAFOD's Statement on Child Labour, 1997; Cambridge University Press for the extract from *Practical Ethics* by Peter Singer, Cambridge University Press, 1993; Diamond Pocket Books, India (www.diamondpocketbooks.com) for the extract from *Rigveda*; The Estate of Carl Sagan for the extract from page 159, of *Billions and Billions* by Carl Sagan; Random House, 1997, copyright © 1997 by the Estate of Carl Sagan; Free the Children for the extracts from 'What is Free the Children?' on www.freethechildren.com; The Islamic Foundation for extracts from *The Qur'an: Basic Teachings* by T. Ballantine Irving, Khurshid Ahmad Muhammad Mawazir, The Islamic Foundation, Leicestershire UK, 1979; the extract from *A Short Introduction to Buddhism* by Damien Keown, Oxford University Press, 2000, © Damien Keown 1996, by permission of Oxford University Press; The Presbyterian Church in Ireland for the extract from *The Tablet*; Reform Synagogues of Great Britain for the extracts from *Forms of Prayer for Jewish Worship, Volume 1, Daily Sabbath Prayer book*, Reform Synagogues of Great Britain, London 1977.

Every effort has been made to trace and acknowledge ownership of copyright. The publishers will be glad to make suitable arrangements with any copyright holders whom it has not been possible to contact.

Orders: please contact Bookpoint Ltd, 130 Milton Park, Abingdon, Oxon OX14 4SB. Telephone: (44) 01235 827720, Fax: (44) 01235 400454. Lines are open from 9.00 – 6.00, Monday to Saturday, with a 24 hour message answering service. Email address: orders@bookpoint.co.uk

British Library Cataloguing in Publication Data
A catalogue record for this title is available from The British Library

ISBN 0 340 781815

First published 2001
Impression number 10 9 8 7 6 5 4 3 2 1
Year   2005 2004 2003 2002 2001

Copyright © 2001 Jim Green (units 3 and 4), Joe Walker (units 1, 2 and 5)

Typeset by Fakenham Photosetting Limited, Fakenham NR21 8NN
Printed in Italy for Hodder & Stoughton Educational, a division of Hodder Headline Plc, 338 Euston Road, London NW1 3BH.

Not all bad news

The United Nations report, A *Vision of Hope* (1995), says that life for most people has become much more 'liveable' and 'probably more fulfilling' during the last 50 years. A lot of progress has been made in dealing with poverty:

- Life expectancy has increased from 46 years to 63.

- The number of children who die before they are five is half what it was 50 years ago.

- Two-thirds of all one-year-olds are now protected against major childhood diseases.

- Developing countries have safe drinking water for 68% of their people and health care for 72%.

What causes poverty?

- If you are born poor, you are more likely to stay poor – especially if you are born in a poor country where opportunities for getting out of poverty are few.

- Some people say that poverty is caused by laziness – not working hard enough. However, many poor people, especially in developing countries, work extremely hard but don't get rewarded properly for their efforts.

- Some people are just lucky. If you are able to take advantage of good circumstances, you can become wealthy.

DISCUSSION POINT

Would you steal if you were hungry? How hungry would you have to be?

The effects of poverty

Poverty can lead to death. It also tends to lead to ill-health and many kinds of social problems. It can change people's behaviour too – perhaps if you were starving you would consider stealing to survive, even if you thought stealing was wrong.

Poverty can make the world less stable. Where whole countries are poor, tension can occur between countries. This can be the cause of war.

DISCUSSION POINT

How far is world poverty everyone's problem?

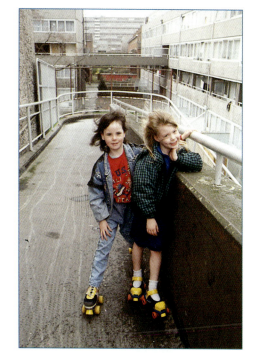

Fig 1.3 Housing takes many forms

Responding to poverty

Some people would argue that poverty is just the way things are, and that nothing can be done about it – nor should it. Some say that we should fight poverty wherever it occurs and whatever the cause – small changes in all our individual lifestyles should be made to help out. Perhaps we could buy FairTrade goods. This is where local producers are paid a fair price for their goods. Profits go to them, not to big foreign-owned companies. Finally, some say that poverty is so serious that we should take action which involves us in great personal sacrifice (like giving away a proportion of our income). Some say that we should use our political power to help the poor, who, they say, have no power.

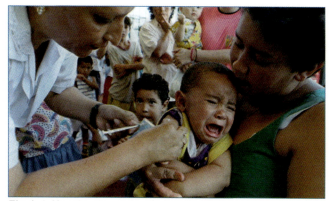

Fig 1.4 Vaccination doesn't cost much

In the **Old Testament** or **Torah**, poverty and hunger are signs that God is not pleased. For example, famines were seen as God's punishment for wickedness. Such teachings led many in the past to ignore poverty. They thought that it could only be solved by the person who was suffering turning to God. The **Tenth Commandment** teaches that it is wrong to be greedy. The **Prophets** taught that poverty was bad, because it was a sign of human greed and unfairness. They called for justice for all – including that everyone should have enough to live a comfortable life. They often pointed out the differences between the 'haves' and the 'have-nots'. They also warned that not helping the poor would lead to punishment.

Fig 1.5 Protesting against poverty

> Therefore because you trample upon the poor and take from him extractions of wheat, you have built houses of hewn stone, but you shall not dwell in them ... For I know how many are your transgressions, and how great your sins – You who afflict the righteous, who take a bribe, and turn aside the needy at the gate.

Amos 5:11–12

Jesus seems to say that wealth is a burden, not a pleasure. He tells a rich man to sell all that he has and give it to the poor. Jesus also teaches his followers to treat the poor as if they were Jesus himself.

> Truly, I say to you, as you did it to one of the least of these my brothers, you did it to me.

Matthew 26:40

The first Christians believed in sharing wealth. In the book of **Acts** there are many teachings about how no-one should be in need. The first Christians made sure that all were treated fairly.

> There was not a needy person among them, those who had land or houses sold them, and brought the proceeds to the apostles; this was distributed to each as any had need.

Acts 2:34–35

Liberation Theology, which began in the slums of South America, argues that you cannot spread the message of **Christianity** while people are hungry and oppressed. A Christian's first responsibility is to help in a practical way.

One of the most important teachings of Christianity is to '**love one another**'. Many Christians believe that the best way to do this is to make sure that people are not poor or hungry.

The **Buddha** taught that food, clothing and shelter were not luxuries but necessities. A story is told of how he refused to teach until his listeners were properly fed, because someone who was starving would not be able to understand the teaching. However, he also taught that wealth had a habit of leading people astray. This was because going after money meant that the search for **enlightenment** would take second place.

However, in **Theravada Buddhism**, the homeless monk is seen as the ideal, because he is able to live without material things.

> Foolish people dread misfortune and strive after good fortune, but those who seek enlightenment must transcend both of them and be free of worldly attachments.

Bukkyo Dendo Kyokai, *The Teaching of Buddha*

Buddhists believe that life involves **dukkha** or suffering. Poverty is a form of suffering. Buddhists feel that it is their duty to help those who are suffering, because by so doing they will:

- build up their own good **karma**, so leading to a better re-birth

- help the suffering person to be able to think more fully about the Buddha's teaching

- act **compassionately** (karuna), which is a key Buddhist belief.

Buddhists believe that helping poor people shows **metta** (loving kindness). By helping the poor, Buddhists also detach themselves from worldly pleasures. This is because, in helping, the Buddhist makes a personal sacrifice by putting the other person first. The Buddhist should help all according to their need:

> Cause the blind, the sick, the lowly, the protectorless, the wretched and the cripple equally to attain food and drink without interruption.

Nagarjuna

Activities

Text Questions

1 What three things do we need to survive?

2 What other things might we need to live a 'full life'?

3 Name two countries in the "North" and two in the "South".

4 State one possible cause of poverty.

5 List two of the possible effects of poverty.

6 In your own words, what does the passage from the Book of Amos teach?

7 What did Jesus tell the rich man to do and why?

8 How did the first Christians help the poor?

9 Why did the Buddha refuse to teach before his listeners had been fed?

10 Why might a Buddhist help the poor?

Discussion Points

● What things do we in rich countries take for granted?

● Why do you think education is important for poor countries?

● Why is having laws important?

● Why do you think so many people in developed countries are overweight?

● What do you think 'being poor' means?

● Why might some countries take advantage of rich ones?

● Do you think poverty can lead to the world being less stable?

● In what ways could we help poor people?

● Are poor people our responsibility?

● Do you think the Buddha was right to want to feed his listeners first?

● Could a Christian argue that it is acceptable to be rich?

Find Out About

● Countries of the world that are rich and poor

● Other North and South differences

● The other problems poverty causes

● Charities that help the poor and how they do so

● How much your government does

● How those with a religious faith help the poor

● Search the web under the heading **FairTrade**. Find out what sorts of products are available and where they come from.

Tasks

1 Work out how many calories you consumed today. Go through your weekly diet. Work out how much of what you eat comes from countries in the South.

2 Produce your own poster encouraging people to help the poor.

3 Write a letter to your local politicians. Tell them what you have learned about world poverty. Ask what their party has done and is going to do about it.

4 Collect images from newspapers and magazines which illustrate 'Rich and Poor'. Create your own collage poster with this title.

5 Write a brief report about the work of one religious organisation which tries to help the poor.

6 Take some photographs of your local area showing the contrasts between rich and poor. Display these in your classroom. Add your own notes to the display.

7 You have won the lottery. You have a deep religious faith. What would you do with your money and why would you do this?

Homework

A Imagine that you become Prime Minister. Write down five things you would do to try to help poor people, either in your own country or abroad. Choose three of these ideas and for each one write one advantage and one disadvantage which might result from putting it into practice.

or

B How might a religious person answer this statement?

'There are poor people in the world – so what? That's nothing to do with me.'

Living in a Material World

Fig 2.1 Poverty on our own streets

Home or away?

One of the important features of poverty in the UK is that there is a clear *contrast* between rich and poor. Britain is a country of extremes – the very rich and the very poor often live side by side. Wealth is also on show a lot – people can tell how new your car is by looking at its number plate! Shops, magazines and television show us expensive goods to buy. If you are poor, it's easy to feel left out, because you can see what you're missing.

Some people say that we should help poor people at home before worrying about those in other countries. 'Charity begins at home' is an old saying about this. Others say that poverty here is as bad as elsewhere in the world – just different.

DISCUSSION POINT

Do you think that poverty in Britain is as bad as in other countries of the world?

You can leave your hat on

One of the major causes of poverty in Britain is unemployment. This not only leads to poverty but to many other effects:

- Communities may be affected if people have to move away from their homes to find work somewhere else.

- Sometimes there's an increase in crime, alcoholism or drug-taking.

- Being out of work often makes people feel powerless and 'left out' of society. This can often lead to problems within families – sometimes violence.

- For some people, their work gives them a sense of identity. Losing a job can be like losing a part of yourself.

Of course, some people cope very well with unemployment – finding new jobs quickly. For many though, unemployment is a major cause of poverty and other problems.

Fig 2.2 One way of escaping poverty?

What to do?

The British government recently announced that it would spend millions of pounds setting up centres in communities so that poor people can get Internet access. The government believes that this will help people get back into work.

There are many job-creation schemes in the UK, and many industries say that they are doing their best to keep people in work. The problem, though, is … us. People who run businesses say that putting people out of work is unavoidable. If we, the customers, want cheaper goods, then we have to accept that this might mean cutting back on workers. If that produces poverty, then what can we do?

There's no place like home

Another important feature of poverty in Britain is homelessness. When did you last pass someone in the street begging? What did you do? Why?

Graham works for the Bethany Trust in Edinburgh. A former drug-addict and prisoner, he was homeless for many years. He now works to help others who are in the same kind of situation he was in.

> 'I became homeless because of family problems. My mum chucked me out when I was 14. Not that she didn't care, she just couldn't cope with a junkie son in her house. I used to sit begging outside Waverley train station. It was interesting the way people reacted to you. Most just fixed their stare straight ahead, refusing to look at you. They'd see you from a long way off and go well out of their way to pass you. Some gave you a kind of sickly smile as they handed you a few coins – others tossed them like they'd given you all their wages. Some though would look at you in a disgusted way. I was even spat on many times. Amazingly this was sometimes done by smart guys in their business suits and briefcases … funny old world.'

There are many reasons why people become homeless, but it's usually a lonely – and often dangerous – life. Some people say that no-one needs to be homeless because of Britain's welfare state. Others say that this doesn't help everyone. Still, some people, particularly some young people, are left homeless and hungry.

Fig 2.3 Spiritually rich but materially poor?

The best things in life are free … ?

Perhaps poverty is all in the mind. Some people argue that real poverty is not when you lack material things, but when you are without friendship, love, freedom and a sense of well-being. If you have little money, but a safe community in which to grow up, your life might be good.

Maybe, in Britain, we focus on material wealth too much. Maybe we think we'll have true happiness when we have lots of 'things'. It is also said that, in countries like Britain, we now spend so much time working to make money to buy things, that we've forgotten how to be contented with 'the simple things'. Your grandparents might tell you that, when they were children, they got an orange and a handful of sweets at Christmas, and they were happy.

On the other hand, some of the wealthiest people don't seem to have found real happiness, despite having everything they could want. In fact, sometimes it looks as if people are never happy with material things because, no matter how much they have, they always want more.

Many of the world's faiths say that being poor is a spiritual thing, not a physical one. They say that, if you are happy with yourself and with life's simple things, then you don't really need material things. So, perhaps what it means to be poor depends upon your point of view.

Focus ▷ Work

The **Christian** faith has always had a keen interest in work. In some ways this is odd because work was God's punishment for Adam's disobedience.

> Because of what you have done, the ground will be under a curse. You will have to work hard all your life to make it produce enough food for you.

Genesis 3:17

For a long time (and, some would say, still) Christians have believed that hard work is something that brings you closer to God. The old saying is that 'the devil makes work for idle hands' – in other words, if you don't work hard, then you might get up to mischief. This has led to what is known as the 'work ethic' where hard work is seen as a sign of living a good life – and avoiding a bad one.

> Be lazy if you want to; sleep on, but you will go hungry.

Proverbs 19:15

However, Christians have been active in helping the unemployed, because of the harmful personal and social effects unemployment can have. They realise that there is a difference between people who don't *want* to work and people who don't have a job through *no fault* of their own.

Christians also believe that work is not just something you do to make money and so buy more things. Wealth, for a Christian, should be spiritual, not material. 'Worldly wealth' is different from 'spiritual wealth':

> If then you have not been faithful in handling worldly wealth, how can you be trusted with true wealth?

Luke 16:11

The **Hindu** caste system is partly based on what type of work you do. The highest form of work, and so highest caste, is professional work, especially priestly duties. These priests are the Brahmins. Those who do the dirtiest work in a society are known as Harijans. This used to mean 'untouchables' but Harijans are now referred to as 'children of God'. So for a Hindu, work is not just what you do, it makes up a part of your identity.

Also, in Hinduism, work is seen as a way of improving yourself spiritually. Doing your **dharma** to the best of your ability is one of the most important ways to build up good karma. This means that you will be able to achieve a better re-birth. Hindus should not use their work simply to achieve a better material life, it should be a way of making spiritual progress.

Hindus believe that life involves various stages. These are the **ashramas**. During each stage of life, some-thing different is expected of you. During the second stage, Grihasthra Ashrama, you are expected to work hard to provide for the needs of your family. The next stage, the Vanaprastha Ashrama, means retiring from work and concentrating on more spiritual matters.

Unemployment is a problem for a Hindu because:

● It means that you can't provide for your family.

● It means that one way of making spiritual progress through life is not available to you.

Humanists believe that work is a way to keep society in order, and also to benefit people. Humanists believe that humans are the highest form of life, and so it is our responsibility to look after ourselves. Humanists would say that effort is good because it makes life easier for everyone – and if we all share work fairly then no-one should be overworked. Humanists would point out that many of the great discoveries and advances in life – like the discovery of medicines – have come through the sheer hard work of the scientists involved.

Unemployment is a problem because it takes away one of the ways in which humans express themselves. It also causes upsets in the balance of social life and welfare. Part of what it means to be human is the need to feel that you are contributing to society – keeping it going and making it better. When you are unem-ployed, you might feel that you aren't helping anyone.

Humanists believe that work can be fulfilling but should not be so drudge-like that it becomes **de-humanising** – making you like a machine instead of a person. Humanists also believe that work practices should be fair and that you should be fairly rewarded for your efforts.

Because Humanists can't turn to a God for help, their own efforts will make – or break – the world in which we live. Striving for better things by our own efforts is a common humanist theme. Work should have a dimension which is not just about material things, but also about 'higher' values.

> But let us compete in finding ways to reverse the nuclear race and to make massive reductions in conventional forces; in eliminating government corruption; in making most of the world agriculturally self-sufficient. Let us vie in art and science, in music and literature, in technological innovation. Let us have an honesty race. Let us compete in relieving suffering and ignorance and disease ...

Carl Sagan, *Billions & Billions*

Activities

Text Questions

1 How can you show that you are wealthy if you live in Britain?

2 What is unemployment?

3 How do some people feel when they are unemployed?

4 How do some businesses explain what causes unemployment?

5 Why did Graham end up homeless?

6 How might you be poor but still happy?

7 What does the phrase 'the devil makes work for idle hands' mean? Do you agree?

8 Which is the highest caste in Hinduism?

9 What do Humanists think is an advantage of work?

Discussion Points

● Where can you see examples in your area of the contrast between rich and poor in Britain?

● Do you agree that 'charity begins at home'?

● Why do you think unemployment can lead to family problems?

● What other problems can unemployment lead to?

● Do you think the government's ideas about Internet access will help unemployed people?

● How do you think people react to the homeless? Why?

● What is the best way to help homeless people?

● Do you agree that the best things in life are free? What are they?

● Do you think that there is a difference between *worldly* and *spiritual* wealth?

● Do you agree that hard work makes you a 'better' person?

Find Out About

● Facts and figures about UK poverty

● The causes of unemployment and its effects on people

● Possible solutions to unemployment

● The causes of homelessness

● Organisations which try to help the homeless, e.g. Shelter

● How world faiths try to help unemployed and homeless people

● Search the web under the heading **UK Government Internet Access Policy**. Find out about the government's ideas about widening Internet access.

Tasks

1 Design and make your own poster showing the contrasts between rich and poor in Britain.

2 Draw up a set of solutions for unemployment. Use your imagination – how could we help people back into work?

3 The characters in *The Full Monty* responded to unemployment in an interesting way. Imagine that you have just lost your job. What would you do? Write about your 'plans'.

4 Imagine that you are homeless and living on the streets. What is life like for you? How do people treat you? Write an imaginary diary for a day, or week, in your life. Try to express your feelings, as well as describing what you do.

5 In Britain in the past, people 'made do'. For example, instead of buying new socks when the old ones got holes in them, they stitched them up. Find out other ways in which people 'made do' in the past.

6 Also in the past, instead of buying toys, children often made them out of 'rubbish'. In groups, gather together some items like old washing-up liquid bottles, boxes, cardboard etc. Now have a class competition to see who can make the most interesting toy out of these objects.

7 Design an information leaflet on the Hindu caste system.

Homework

A You are a follower of a world faith. You find yourself walking past a homeless person begging on the street. You stop yourself. Do you give some money? Explain what you would do and why. How do your beliefs affect your actions?

or

B Find out two ways in which the government tries to help poor people. How helpful do you think these are?

I.O.U.

Money makes the world go round

When a country faces financial problems it might borrow money. This leaves it in debt, and paying back what it owes can sometimes keep it in poverty instead of helping it. Comic Relief raised £26 million in 1997. Africa was paying more than this back every day in debt repayments.

At the end of 1999, British Chancellor Gordon Brown cancelled the majority of third world debt owed to Britain. He called the debt the start of a 'virtuous circle', and said it is a 'burden imposed from the past on the present'. His actions may have been a response to the Jubilee 2000 campaign. This organisation campaigned hard for developed countries to cancel the debt owed to them by the developing world.

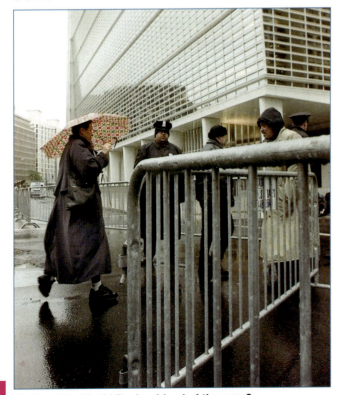

Fig 3.1 The World Bank – friend of the poor?

Perhaps people in the twenty-first century are beginning to look at money in a different way – or perhaps not.

DISCUSSION POINT

Why might a poor country borrow money?

Helping hand or under the thumb?

Debts may be owed to richer countries, the World Bank or the International Monetary Fund (IMF). The World Bank was set up in 1944 to help countries which were struggling economically. It now has 178 members and they vote according to how much money they contribute. The same happens with the IMF, an organisation of the United Nations (UN). This means that the process of giving out financial help and making sure it is repaid is controlled by the world's wealthy nations – particularly Japan, France, Germany, the UK and the USA. Depending upon your point of view, these organisations either help out poor nations as a last resort or keep poor nations dependent on richer ones.

DISCUSSION POINT

Should votes in these organisations be related to how much money a country contributes? Why? Why not?

Strings

Sometimes these organisations instruct the countries receiving financial help to make changes in the way their country is run. These are called Structural Adjustment Policies (SAPs). The poor country is told to make changes which should make it more competitive in the world economy. The idea is that this will attract businesses and create work for local people. This should mean that, as the country gets wealthier, the benefits 'trickle down' to the poor.

Unfortunately, sometimes these SAPs harm the poor. For example, as governments try to build up their economies, they may cut spending on things like health and education. It can also mean that the country has to sell its products to wealthy countries. Manufacturing might be at the expense of feeding its own people, who also cannot afford to buy expensive products which come from the richer countries! A lot of the money given to help goes back to the rich countries as interest payments on the original loans! Perhaps this kind of help has too many strings attached.

DISCUSSION POINT

Are such 'strings' necessary?

Fig 3.2 A frenzy of buying and selling

World markets

The world's trading markets can also present problems for the world's poor. Anything which is traded is known as a commodity (for example foods or resources to produce other things). The price of these commodities can rise and fall quickly, and by large amounts. Richer countries can control this because the price is related to how much they are prepared to pay. For the ordinary producer, this can be very serious because how much they get for their produce can change from day to day. They might even get less for their goods than they cost to produce. Also, poorer countries might find that they can afford to buy something like oil today, but that by tomorrow it will be too expensive. Organisations like

FairTrade try to even out these ups and downs by paying fair and regular prices for produce from the developing world. Some people see this as the right thing to do, others disagree. Some say that you should take advantages when you can, even if this means the poor suffer. That's business, after all.

DISCUSSION POINT

How might changes in prices affect poor producers?

Digging up the root of all evil

In Christianity, money used to be seen as the source of all bad, because if you cared too much about it you would care too little about anything else. Dom Helder Camara, a Christian priest, said;

'I used to think that Christ was exaggerating when he warned about the dangers of wealth. Today I know better … Money has a dangerous way of freezing people's hands, eyes, lips and hearts.'

Many people today make 'ethical investments'. This might mean that they put their money into banks where it can be 'used' to help the poor. Others use their money to make a point – like buying FairTrade products.

Most religions teach that money is something to watch out for, because it is powerful and can cause problems – even for its owners.

DISCUSSION POINT

What problems might having money cause for you?

Fig 3.3 Life on the factory floor can be harsh

Buddhists believe that someone who chases after wealth is like a child who licks honey from the blade of a knife. While he is enjoying the sweetness he risks hurting his tongue. Anyone who 'clings' to wealth will be unhappy, because the things which wealth can bring are only temporary.

The **Buddha** taught that one should work hard and use the wealth gained wisely. He warned that you should not become a slave to wealth, but nor should you ignore it. The Buddha's **middle way** means that you should aim to be neither too wealthy nor too poor. Wealth, gained by **righteous** means, is not something to be ashamed of but to be used for the benefit of others. Being wealthy is only a problem if it makes you selfish and if you become attached to money for its own sake.

Muslims believe that wealth is a gift from Allah, to be used wisely:

Neither give too lavishly, nor yet hold back, and keep a happy medium …

Surah 25:67 (a Surah is a verse from the Qur'an)

Money is not to be made for its own sake, because this can be dangerous:

How awful it will be for every backbiting slanderer who amasses wealth and keeps on counting it. He thinks his wealth will make him immortal. Nevertheless he will be flung into [Hell].

Surah 104:1–5

Muslims believe that some people are made wealthy by Allah. How they use their money is a test for them:

He … has raised some of you higher than others in rank so that He may test you by means of what He has given you.

Surah 6:165

However, Muslims should not gain **interest** on their money:

Allah has permitted trading and forbidden interest.

Surah 2:275

Many wealthy Muslims carry out acts of charity. This shows that they are aware that money is a gift from Allah which he has given them to use sensibly on his behalf. How well they carry out this job will be taken into account by Allah when he judges them.

One of the five pillars is **zakah**. This means giving 2.5% of your wealth to the poor every year. This both helps them and helps you to become less attached to your wealth. For Muslims, you cannot call yourself a believer unless you help the poor:

Have you seen someone who rejects religion? That is the person who pushes the orphan aside and does not encourage feeding the needy.

Surah 107:1–3

Jews too believe that money is to be used wisely. You should see it as a temporary benefit. The **Mishnah** states:

When a man leaves this world, neither silver nor gold … may accompany him, but only the scriptures he has learned and the good works he has carried out.

Don't be upset when a man becomes rich … he cannot take it with him when he dies.

Psalm 49

Jews believe in giving **tzedakah** (money) and **gemilat chassadim** (time and effort) to help poor people. Jews are forbidden from taking interest from other Jews (Exodus 22:24) but are allowed to take it from non-Jews (Deuteronomy 23:20–21).

A Jewish organisation, **Mazon** (food) raises money from Jews in the USA by allowing them to donate 3% of the cost of weddings, bar mitzvahs and other happy occasions. It then uses this money to provide cash grants to help those working with the poor, whether or not they are Jewish. This follows an old Jewish tradition where landowners would leave a corner of their fields for poor people, as well as the Jewish idea of inviting the poor to share in meals on the Shabbat and other holy days. Jews see this as part of the Jewish ideal of **tikkun olam** – repairing the world. Jews see wealth as a blessing from God, but one which is to be used for the good of all – not just some. Wealth is to be seen as a benefit, but caring for it too much will make it a burden:

If you love money, you will never be satisfied; if you long to be rich, you will never get all you want … The richer you are the more mouths you must feed … A rich man has so much [money] that he just stays awake worrying.

Ecclesiastes 5:10–12

Jesus pointed out the dangers of money when he told the rich young ruler to go and sell all he had (Mark 10:21). He made it clear that it was more important to build up riches in heaven rather than on earth.

Activities

Text Questions

1 What is a debt?

2 Which countries have most say in the work of the World Bank and the IMF?

3 What is a Structural Adjustment Policy?

4 What do some people see as the disadvantages of Structural Adjustment Policies?

5 What is a commodity?

6 What did Dom Helder Camara say about wealth? Do you agree?

7 What is an ethical investment?

8 When do Buddhists believe that being wealthy can be 'a problem'?

9 What do Muslims believe about charging interest?

10 What two things do Jews think you should give to the poor?

Discussion Points

- Why do you think Chancellor Gordon Brown cancelled third world debt? Was he right to do so?

- What do you think he meant by the phrase 'virtuous circle'?

- What are the advantages and disadvantages of organisations like the IMF?

- Do you think the benefits of aid always reach the poor?

- Why do the prices of commodities rise and fall so quickly?

- Should we take advantage of the poor?

- How can money be 'the root of all bad'? Do you think it is?

- What do you think Buddhists mean by 'righteous means'?

- What things might a Jew do to give gemilat chassadim to the poor?

Find Out About

- Countries which are in debt today, who to, and what effects this has

- The conditions that are usually attached to Structural Adjustment Policies

- How the commodities market works

- The work of FairTrade and other similar organisations

- The work of Muslim Aid

- Search the web under the heading **Jubilee 2000 Coalition**. Find out about the Campaign to cancel world debt.

Tasks

1 Prepare your own display board on the work of FairTrade and similar organisations. Show the ways in which these organisations claim to help local producers in the developing world. Include written work, artwork, photos etc. You will find that FairTrade product packaging usually carries a lot of information.

2 Do a survey of your local supermarket. How much of the produce there comes from developing world countries? How much is traded 'fairly'? Perhaps you could ask the manager of the supermarket for his or her comments on the findings of your survey.

3 You will have to do some careful research for the following activity. As a class, imagine you are a meeting of the IMF. A developing world country has asked for a loan. Discuss whether you will grant it or not, and what conditions will be attached to it. Individual members of your class should speak for different countries. This means they'll have to find out about that country to start with! Take a vote at the end.

4 Draw up a chart of spending habits. For every person in the class note down how much they spend every week and what on. Be sensitive to each other when doing this and allow people not to take part if they don't want to. Display the chart in your classroom. Perhaps if you have e-mail, you could exchange your findings with pupils in other schools in other countries, including developing countries. You could then display these findings in the classroom.

5 Write to your local Church, Mosque, Synagogue or other holy building. Ask what they teach about the use of money. Display your findings in the classroom.

6 Many faiths believe in judgement after death. If you died today, how would you be judged for your use of money? Draw up a table which shows 'good' things you do with your money and 'bad' things. How did you do?

Homework

A For one world faith, write an explanation of its views on wealth. Aim your writing at someone who doesn't know much about that faith.

or

B Using newspapers and magazines, cut out images which illustrate the topic of money, especially how it is used and abused.

Suffer the Children

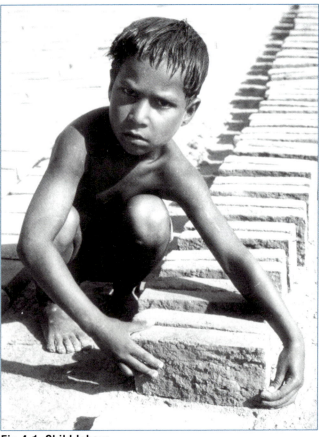

Fig 4.1 Child labour

Children first?

Most societies agree that children are important, though children may be the first to lose out when poverty strikes. In the developing world, children often have to work. Their jobs are not like a child in Britain might have – for example a paper round. These jobs are often dangerous, exhausting and take up most of the child's day. In Britain, many children 'work' unofficially as carers for sick parents, or to babysit younger brothers and sisters. These carers are often kept off school and so miss out on an education.

Slavery in the twenty-first century

We often think of slavery as something from the past, but in some countries today there are 'debt slaves'. A debt slave is a person who works to pay off a debt owed. Sometimes the interest rates are so high that the debt is never repaid. This means that the person has to keep working without limit, really becoming a slave. This is sometimes known as 'bonded labour'. It is not illegal to sell your labour to repay a debt, but it is illegal if the terms of that debt are not clear.

Often such debt slaves are children. This is because they are easy to control and can often do delicate work better than adults. Also, some families are so poor that they sell their children for cash, or 'loan' them out. These children are often ill-treated. Sometimes they become part of the sex industry, working as prostitutes. Of course, this doesn't just happen in the developing world. Child prostitution is said to be on the increase in Britain too.

Article 32 of the United Nations Convention on the Rights of the Child states that, although children can work, this work should not affect their education or harm the child's 'physical, mental, spiritual, moral or social development'. Most slavery of this kind happens in the developing world – but not all.

Fig 4.2 Pocket money or survival?

DISCUSSION POINT

In what ways might the rights of children be a particularly important issue?

Child poverty in the developed world

The National Center for Children in Poverty (NCCP) in the USA – one of the richest countries in the world, and probably the most powerful – claims that the number of American young children living in poverty increased from 3.5 million in 1979 to 5.2 million in 1997. This means that 22% of young children in the USA live in poverty, and 10% live in extreme poverty. Just as serious is the claim that 42% of all American children under six years old live in situations which are 'near poverty'. Many say that the situation is no different here in Britain.

A straightforward issue?

The Catholic Fund for Overseas Development (CAFOD) said in October 1997 that child labour was not a simple issue. Although it agrees that work should never be dangerous or exploit the child, it does sometimes think there are benefits:

> Take a typical example – a ten-year-old girl selling newspapers in the morning traffic of a large city. She runs risks: to her health from pollution or accidents; to her education in terms of lost schooling or exhaustion; to her future in

exposure to street crime or drugs. On the other hand she benefits: the money she earns may help pay her way through school in the afternoons: she may eat more or be treated better in her home because of the income she brings in: her status as a breadwinner brings her self-confidence.

Taking the initiative

The organisation Free the Children aims to:

> Free children from poverty, exploitation and abuse ... [and] ... give children a voice, ... to take action on issues which affect them from a local to an international level.

It is run by children. Only children who are *under* 18 are allowed to vote on decisions or act as spokespersons. Any adults who work for this organisation have to understand that adults are only there to help out. Among its many achievements it has bought farming land for '15 fatherless families' in Nicaragua, so that the families can send their children to school instead of working. It has raised over $100,000 to build a centre for freed bonded child labourers in Alwar, India. It even convinced a group of teachers in Brazil to give up their free time to teach child workers basic reading and writing skills.

Fig 4.3 Street children

In Makkah, before the arrival of **Islam**, families would sometimes kill their own children because they could not afford to keep them. The prophet **Muhammad** taught that this was very wrong because Allah would provide for them:

> Do not kill your children because of poverty; We shall provide for you as well as for them.

Surah 6:151

Children were not to be exploited. Instead, Muhammad taught that they should be looked after, until they were old enough to look after themselves. No-one was to live off their efforts. If they did, then a great punishment awaited them:

> Those who live on orphan's property without having any right to do so will only suck up fire into their bellies, and they will eventually roast in a blaze.

Surah 4:10

Muslims believe that helping the poor is a way of showing their **obedience** to Allah, not for any personal reward:

> They offer food to the needy … out of love for Him: 'We are only feeding you for God's sake. We want no reward from you nor any thanks.'

Surah 76:8–9

Muslims think of children as 'a trial' (Surah 8:28), meaning that how we treat them will be **judged** by Allah, and punished or rewarded accordingly.

Sikhs believe that attachment to worldly things holds you back from true **enlightenment**. Helping the poor (**vand cako**) is probably the best way to free yourself from wrong beliefs and actions. This will ensure spiritual progress. A story is told:

Duni Chand, a wealthy man, invited Guru Nanak to his home. The Guru gave him a needle, telling Duni Chand to return it to him in the next world. Chand's wife laughed, so he asked the Guru how this was possible – what could he take beyond death? The Guru replied: 'Good deeds. Feed the hungry, clothe the naked, house the poor.'

Sikhs should give a tenth of their surplus wealth to charity. This is known as **daswandh**, and brings merit. Sikhs should also work for the poor whenever possible:

> If we want to get a seat in the court of God, we should dedicate ourselves in this world to the service of the people.

Adi Granth 26

Sikhs are forbidden from living off the work of others. This means that they should not benefit from child labour. Guru Nanak said that anyone who lives off the efforts of others lives a sinful life. Sikhs stress the importance of **sewa**, selfless service. Part of this is the **langar**, the free kitchen where food is distributed after worship to everyone who wants it.

The value of children to **Jesus** is clear. In Mark 10:13–16, Jesus welcomes the children. His disciples try to turn them away because they feel Jesus is too tired. Jesus replies:

> Let the children come to me and do not stop them, because the Kingdom of God belongs to such as these.

Christians see children as a blessing from God, and not to be mistreated.

In most world faiths, children are thought of as especially important. This is because they are the future generation, and the survival of a faith and its way of life depends on them. If the children give up their faith, then the faith could end completely.

Many faiths work very hard to include children in all their special activities and religious festivals.

Activities

Text Questions

1 What is a 'debt slave'?

2 What other phrase is used to describe a debt slave?

3 Why are children often used as debt slaves?

4 When might a family 'sell' a child?

5 What does Article 32 of the United Nations Convention on the Rights of the Child state?

6 What is CAFOD, and what does it believe about child labour?

7 What percentage of children live in poverty in the USA according to the NCCP?

8 Do you think child prostitution is different to any other kind?

9 What is unusual about the organisation Free the Children?

10 What does Surah 107:1–3 teach about helping the poor?

11 What do Muslims believe will happen to those who live off the efforts of others?

12 What do Sikhs believe you can take beyond death?

13 Why are children so important for many world faiths?

Discussion Points

- What benefits can working bring a child?

- Do you think there should be age limits on work, or on certain types of work?

- What do you think should happen to people who sell their children, or loan them out?

- How might work affect your 'physical, mental, spiritual, moral and social development'?

- Is child poverty in the developed world any different to that in the developing world?

- Why might Free the Children have taken the approach it has?

- Do you think child poverty is any more serious than any other kind of poverty?

- What are the benefits and drawbacks of zakah?

- Why do you think Sikhs want to help the poor?

- In what ways might children be considered 'a blessing'?

Find Out About

- The work of the Anti-Slavery Society
- Other forms of child labour
- UNICEF
- The extent of child poverty in the UK
- Other organisations which try to help children – especially those within world faiths
- Search the web under the heading **Children in Poverty**. Find out about some of the organisations that are trying to fight this problem.

Tasks

1 Run your own class debate on the following issue: 'Children should not be allowed to work before they are 16, no matter where they live.'

2 Prepare a display for your classroom which shows how, where and why children work around the world. You should particularly highlight examples of children in bonded labour situations. Also, you should try to balance up the treatment of children in the developed world with the treatment of children in the developing world.

3 Imagine you woke up tomorrow to find yourself as a Brazilian street child. You are alone and hungry and have to work on the streets to survive. Write an imaginative story about a day in your life.

4 Draw up a Children's Charter. List 10 basic rights you think a child should have, and state some ways in which you might help bring them about. Display this in your classroom. Once you have done this you should compare it with the UN declaration on the Rights of the Child, and with similar declarations from other organisations.

5 Perhaps you could find out more about how you could help children who live in poverty. As a result of your studies your class could organise an event to raise money for a children's charity at home or abroad.

6 Find out the ways in which world faiths include their children in their activities. You could talk about or display your findings.

Homework

A Design and make an information leaflet which illustrates the theme 'Child Poverty Today'. Try to include some of the teachings of different religions on the issue.

or

B Design a poster on the theme of 'Child Slavery'.

What a Relief

To help or not

A speaker at the World Council of Churches in 1975 said: The rich must live more simply so that the poor can simply live.' Although there are disagreements about how best to help the poor, most agree that we should. Some help because they think it's right, others to make themselves feel better, and still others because they worry about what might happen to the world if they don't. Some don't notice and some pretend not to. Some don't think it is their concern. The question is this: is allowing the poor to die when we can do something to stop it the same as killing someone?

First aid or Band Aid?

Apart from direct financial aid to the developing world, or aid in the form of debt relief, there are many other ways in which help can be given:

- technical assistance – giving technical help so that developing countries can industrialise more quickly, or training locals in new technology

- programme aid – supporting developing countries in the international markets

- project aid – financing and supporting specific projects to help a country develop

- tied aid – allowing a developing country 'special deals' when buying products from a developed country.

For most developed countries aid has, on average, been around 0.3% of their wealth per year. Some see this as a drop in the ocean, others as better than nothing. Critics of aid say that it just keeps poor countries down. There is also imbalance; from 1983 to 1990, the developing world paid the developed world $160 billion. Aid to the developing world was around $52 billion. There are also those who say that most aid is like a sticking plaster – it helps for a while, but works its way off and needs to be replaced.

The sheer number of aid agencies run by developing world governments is staggering – the IBRD, ICPD, IDA, ODA, IFAD, IMF, are just a few. Most developed world governments also have their own overseas aid departments. Someone once suggested that the money spent on running all these organisations would get at least one small African country completely out of its problems.

Fig 5.1 Charity begins at home?

DISCUSSION POINT

Do you think the developed world does enough to help the poor?

Of course, the developing world sometimes doesn't help itself. Many developing countries are accused of wasting their aid through corruption and poor organisation. Also, aid can be swallowed up in funding local wars.

Direct action

There are many voluntary organisations which try to stop poverty in their own countries and in the developing world. These organisations depend entirely on public support for their work. They raise money through collections, sponsored events, appeals, by selling developing world goods, as well as through second-hand shops and donations. In 1942, the Oxford Committee for Famine Relief was set up. It is now known as OXFAM and is one of the biggest poverty relief organisations in the world. There are others: Save the Children, Help the Aged, Christian Aid, Muslim Aid, Shelter. Many of these organisations have been on the go for some time. Their aims are to help those in poverty by giving them the means to support themselves. They believe that the poor need to be given opportunities. As well as emergency relief programmes – for example after the effects of floods or famines – they do long-term work with the poor. This might be by providing clean water sources or by building schools. All of these give local people the chance to take control of their own lives.

DISCUSSION POINT

Why do you think people give to charities such as these?

Give us your F!*^@#$ money!

On 13 July 1985, Bob Geldof's Live Aid concert urged us to 'Feed the World'.

> I stood stock still, my hand raised above me ... in unconscious salute ... In front of me stood 80,000 people. Somewhere, invisible, behind them, another billion people all over the world had joined us ... Together we held our breath ... Throughout Africa on this day people were starving ...

Bob Geldof, Is That It?

This concert was in aid of a terrible famine in Ethiopia. The famine was brought vividly to the television screens of millions in the developed world. TV had allowed us to glimpse what poverty really meant as it happened. Bob Geldof famously swore on the BBC, by urging everyone just to 'give us your F!*^@#$ money'. Live Aid went on to raise huge amounts of money. Comic Relief followed, as did many other songs and concerts which gave their proceeds to charity. TV charity 'marathons' like Children in Need are now regular events in the UK. Comic Relief's Red Nose Day now takes place every few years. At the end of the twentieth century a massive campaign saw many people giving their last hour's wages to charity.

Poverty relief has now entered the technological twenty-first century. A scan through the Internet will show that poverty relief organisations, old and new, are now using the most up-to-date technologies in their efforts to help the poor.

DISCUSSION POINT

Do you think you will ever live in a world where there is no poverty?

Fig 5.2 A well-known British way of helping out

Focus — Beliefs into action

The **Salvation Army** claims to be '**Christianity with its sleeves rolled up**'. Since 1887, when its founder, William Booth saw people sleeping rough on the streets of London, it has 'gone and done something' for the world's poor. Booth believed that there was no point in preaching to someone about Jesus if that person needed practical help first. A week after Booth first realised how poor some people were, his Salvation Army was already feeding 2000 people. Today, the extent of the Salvation Army's work is astounding. In **Britain** it runs:

- 50 hostels offering 3355 beds
- five centres to help alcoholics
- three residential community homes for children in need

In **other countries** it runs:

- 800 hostels for the poor
- 2100 food distribution centres
- 202 children's homes

In all, it helps 2.5 million families every year. The Salvation Army believes that it is putting into practice the teaching of Jesus:

I was hungry and you fed me, thirsty and you gave me a drink, I was a stranger and you received me in your homes, naked and you clothed me; I was sick and you took care of me . . .

The righteous will answer him, 'When Lord did we see you hungry and feed you, or thirsty and give you a drink?' . . .

The king will reply, 'I tell you, whenever you did this for one of the least important of these brothers of mine, you did it for me.'

Matthew 25:35–40

Salvationists see Jesus in everyone they help.

Islamic Relief, based in Birmingham, was founded in 1984. Its aims are to:

- reduce poverty and the causes of poverty
- provide emergency aid when needed
- help those in need.

This organisation has projects on the go in over 22 countries across the world. It states that its actions are a form of **sadaqah** – charity. Such sadaqah has two functions: to show **submission** to Allah, and also to show care for other people. It quotes Surah 3:92 in support of its work:

You shall not attain righteousness unless you spend on others that which you love, and whatever you spend truly Allah knows.

Helping others is seen as a way of **purifying** yourself from the problems which come with being too attached to wealth. The Hadith goes further by saying:

He is not a believer who eats while his neighbour remains hungry by his side.

Another organisation, **Muslim Aid** raised over £2.5 million in 1998.

The organisation **War on Want** is a non-religious organisation. It started in 1951 and was founded by Harold Wilson and Victor Gollancz. It claims that its role is to:

Challenge the powerful and help the dispossessed fight back.

The aim of War on Want is to tackle the **causes** of poverty as well as the effects. Although it helps abroad as well as at home, it thinks that it is important not to;

Preach or send experts to tell people how things should be done. We just give much needed support and listen to what they want.

Its Vice President, Roy Hattersley, said:

'War on Want exists because in the developing world there is a need. The need is for solidarity not charity. For a hand-up not a hand-out. For an end to the root causes of poverty and not just its symptoms.'

War on Want reflects many non-religious viewpoints because it concerns itself with human need and suggests that the only way to respond to that need is through human action. This reflects the beliefs of **Humanists** who would argue that the solution to world poverty lies in our own hands.

Perhaps it is more important to be politically active in the interests of the poor than to give to them oneself – but why not do both?

Peter Singer, *Practical Ethics*

Activities

Text Questions

1 What did the speaker say at the World Council of Churches in 1975? What do you think he meant?

2 State two ways in which aid can be given to the developing world.

3 How much of their wealth every year do developed countries give, on average, to the developing world?

4 In what ways do developing countries sometimes not 'help themselves'?

5 How do voluntary organisations raise their money?

6 What kinds of things do these voluntary organisations do?

7 What did Bob Geldof say on TV and why? Do you think he was right to do so?

8 What was Live Aid?

9 What kind of work does the Salvation Army do?

10 What is sadaqah?

11 What are the aims of War on Want?

12 Do you think that British people should support British charities before helping people in other countries?

Discussion Points

● Why do you think some people choose to help the poor and others do not?

● What kind of aid do you think is likely to be most successful?

● Do you think aid today is just a 'band aid'?

● Do you think helping the poor to build schools is as important as making sure they have clean water?

● Do you think rock concerts and charity songs are a good way to help the poor?

● How might the Internet benefit charity organisations?

● What might a Salvationist mean by saying that he 'sees Jesus in the poor'?

● How might sadaqah show submission to Allah?

● Do you agree that the poor need 'solidarity not charity'?

Find Out About

● Types of aid to the developing world – their benefits and drawbacks

● Oxfam's work

● The work of other voluntary aid agencies

● How the Live Aid concert came about

● Comic Relief

● Search the web under the heading **BBC Children in Need**. Find out how much the latest appeal raised and some of the things the money was spent on.

Tasks

1 Produce your own class quotes board. On this board you should include quotes from some of the topics you have studied in this book, as well as some comments made by pupils in your class as you have gone through the materials. You may like to illustrate some of these quotes for display in your classroom.

2 You may like to try making your own short TV commercial about an aspect of the topics you have studied. It is only recently that charities have been allowed to advertise on TV. How would you draw people's attention to the plight of the world's poor and what would you expect them to do about it?

3 Imagine Live Aid were to take place today. Who would be in it? Perhaps you could draw up a programme for your own fantasy concert!

4 Choose one of the aid agencies you have found out about. Invite a speaker to your class to talk about their work. Produce a series of questions you would like to ask them.

5 What could the Salvation Army do in your area? Draw up a list of jobs for them to do.

6 Design your own piece of artwork to match the text in Matthew 25:35–40.

7 Work out a way in which your class or your school could help the poor.

Homework

A Write answers to the following:

● What have you learned about world poverty from this book?

● How has it changed your attitudes to world poverty?

● What would you still like to know about world poverty?

or

B Draw up two lists as follows:

● Three things I could do to help the world's poor

● Three things my country could do

Introduction to Human Rights

What rights?

Your teacher tells you to ballet dance for the class. You refuse. You are punished. Fair? Most people probably wouldn't think so. Your teacher has the 'right' to tell you to do certain things and not others. How do we decide what those things are? Are there basic human rights which we all share? Where do those rights come from and who decides what they are?

DISCUSSION POINT

What things do you think your teacher should and should not be able to tell you to do?

Rights for all

On 10 December 1948, the United Nations issued its 'Universal Declaration of Human Rights'. This set of guidelines is meant to suggest what everyone on Earth should expect as their right, whoever or wherever they are. In its opening statement it says:

● There are basic rights which everyone should enjoy (*inalienable rights*).

● Not having rights leads to 'barbarous acts'.

● Rights should be protected by the law.

● If all the countries of the world accepted such rights then the world would be a better place.

The declaration includes 30 different statements (Articles) about what rights everyone should be able to expect. All of these are based on two simple ideas:

All human beings are born free and equal in dignity and rights.

Article I

Everyone has the right to life, liberty and security of person.

Article 3

DISCUSSION POINT

What do you think these statements mean? Do you agree?

Fig 6.1 Keeping the peace

Force or persuasion?

All 184 countries which are members of the UN have agreed to these human rights. They should try to uphold them in their own lands. When these Articles are broken, the international community often steps in and tries to force or persuade countries to apply them. Sometimes, this can lead to conflict. Attempts to restore basic human rights are not always successful. The problem is that there are many ways of breaking these Articles.

Sometimes a country breaks many of them at once during war situations or civil unrest. Other times it repeatedly breaks one or several Articles. Occasionally just one is broken. For example, the treatment of civilians by Russia during the conflict in Chechnya was criticised by the UN, but then Britain's treatment of 'political prisoners' in Northern Ireland has been attacked by organisations such as Amnesty International. Perhaps there should be different ways of dealing with these *infringements* of human rights.

Fig 6.2 Free speech – always right?

Doing what you want

Imagine a world where anyone could do whatever they wanted. Life would be dangerous. We all agree that there are rules we should all follow for our own good. Everyone likes freedom, but we accept that our freedom to do what we want should respect other people's rights. Sometimes this means we have to do things we'd rather not for other people's (and so our own) good. If there were no rules, then I'd just have to look out for myself – too bad if I'm weak. This is called anarchy.

Human rights exist to protect the weak against the misuse of power by the strong. Perhaps human rights need to be there to protect us all against human nature.

Conflicts of rights

The problem comes when there are different ideas about what rights we should have, and how to enforce these rights. For example, I might support everyone's right to free speech. However, suppose a group of people who believe that black people are inferior want to march through my street. Should I support their right to do so? What if my government supported their right and used the police to protect such a march? Would I break the law in protest?

DISCUSSION POINT

Are all rights equally important?

In Austria recently, a government was elected which has strong views about foreigners in Austria. People around the world have protested – do they have the right to do so? Should the Austrian government resign?

Human rights 'abuses' often happen when a government, or a group of people, sees a group or individual as somehow a 'threat' to their way of life – what one person calls a terrorist, another calls a freedom fighter. In the same way that we limit our own freedom so that our actions don't harm others, a government might say that it is doing the same when it punishes, imprisons or executes someone. It might say that the action is not an abuse of human rights, but one which protects the country.

Human nature

Maybe disagreements about rights are just a part of human nature which we can't avoid. Maybe there are no 'inalienable rights'. Perhaps competition among humans for survival means that we can only give others 'rights' which are in our own interest. Maybe, as some religions say, we should be able to put others first and limit our own freedom for the good of all. Maybe there are some basic human rights about which we should all agree. Maybe not.

DISCUSSION POINT

Do you agree that there are some human rights which everyone should enjoy? If so, what are they?

Fig 6.3 The Maze prison – political prisoners?

Christians believe that all humans deserve respect and fair treatment because they belong to God. People are made in God's image, and so to treat God's creation badly is the same as being disrespectful to God (Genesis 2:7).

In the **Old Testament**, there is a long tradition of speaking out against injustice:

> [The Lord] judges in favour of the oppressed and gives food to the hungry.
>
> The Lord sets prisoners free and gives sight to the blind. He lifts those who have fallen ...
>
> but ruins the plans of the wicked.
>
> Psalm 146

The **Prophets** spent much of their time criticising rulers for their poor treatment of ordinary people and told them they should put an end to it or suffer at God's hands. They also argued that wickedness was based on wrong beliefs (see Jer 17:5–9). When people turned back to God, everything would be all right. Christians can take one of two approaches to human rights:

- Some believe that **Jesus'** command to 'love one another' should be put into practical action. This means protesting about human rights abuses and trying to help directly those who are suffering.

- Others believe that the priority is to teach people to turn to God, not to take part in 'politics'. When people have a good relationship with God, there will be no more human rights abuses.

Most Christians would probably point to the parable of the **Good Samaritan** (Luke 10:25–37) as the best example of Christian teaching about human rights. Here, a Samaritan, arch-enemy of the Jews, helps an unknown Jew who has been beaten up and left for dead. This combines both proper action and right belief. Christians believe that to follow Jesus means to help others as if they were Jesus himself.

Jews use the Prophets as examples of what should be done when human rights are threatened. They believe that turning back to God will produce improvements in how we treat each other (see Isaiah 1:18). Beliefs *and* actions have consequences:

> Your reward depends upon what you say and what you do; you will get what you deserve.
>
> Prov 12:14

However, in the meantime we should do what we can to help those in need. Judaism has its own 'declaration of human rights' in the form of the **Ten Commandments** (Exodus 20:2–17). Many of these commandments could be rewritten as statements of human rights:

- *Observe the Sabbath:* everyone has the right to a day of rest from work

- *Do not kill:* everyone has the right to life

- *Do not commit adultery:* everyone has the right to be cared for in a relationship

- *Do not steal:* everyone's property should be respected

- *Do not accuse anyone falsely:* everyone has the right to a fair trial

- *Respect your father and mother*: everyone has the right to be treated respectfully

Many people say that modern declarations of human rights are partly based on rules such as the Ten Commandments.

Jews also follow other **mitzvoth** (commandments), many of which have to do with their treatment of others. As the **chosen people**, Jews believe that they are God's special representatives on Earth. How they behave should be an example for others to follow. Such a serious responsibility means that they have to be careful about how they treat others – because others might follow their example.

Buddhists believe that all life should be respected. All living beings have a 'Buddha-nature'. This means they have the potential to become enlightened. Therefore, they must be treated with consideration and given basic human rights. If not, then we are putting obstacles in their way which may harm their chances of becoming enlightened.

Activities

Text Questions

1 When did the UN issue its 'Declaration of Human Rights'?

2 Who does it suggest should be given these rights?

3 How should these rights be protected?

4 What might the UN do when a country infringes any of the 30 Articles?

5 Why did the UN criticise Russia's activities in Chechnya?

6 Why has Britain been criticised by Amnesty International?

7 Why do we sometimes choose not to do what we want?

8 Why have people protested about the Austrian government?

9 How might a government argue that its actions are not abuses of human rights?

10 Why might a Christian believe that he should not get involved in politics?

11 Why might a Jew think how he behaves is especially important?

Discussion Points

- What basic human rights do you think we should all enjoy?

- Why do you think the UN issued its declaration *when* it did?

- Are all people born equal? Should they be?

- How can the lack of human rights lead to 'barbarous acts'?

- Does the UN have the right to interfere in a country's business?

- What does it mean to say that 'perhaps human rights need to be there to protect us against human nature'? Do you agree?

- How would you react to a racist march through your street?

- Are abuses of human rights unavoidable?

- Are Christians right to take part in politics?

- Do the ten commandments still apply today?

Find Out About

- The rights your teacher has

- The UN Declaration of Human Rights

- The work of the UN

- The rights of governments and the rights of the individual

- The arguments given by one 'terrorist' organisation

- Ways in which Christians and Jews have been involved in human rights issues

- The conflicts in Israel and Palestine over human rights

- Search the web under the heading **Amnesty International**. Find out about Amnesty's work.

Tasks

1 Get hold of a copy of the UN Declaration. Write the 30 Articles out for class display. For each one include one image which shows how this article is being kept today, and one which shows how it is being broken.

2 Using a world map, stick pins into countries which are accused of human rights abuses. Join these pins by string to your own written descriptions of what it is claimed is happening there.

3 Draw up your own 'Declaration of the Rights of the Pupil'. Then draw up your own 'Declaration of the Responsibilities of the Pupil'. Display these in your school.

4 Choose two specific human rights issues and design an information poster about them. Show what the issues are, and how these rights are abused today.

5 Run a short class debate: 'It is the right of a government to protect its people any way it wants.'

6 You are a religious person. You have read in the paper a letter which tells religious people to 'keep their nose out of politics because it doesn't concern them'. Write a response.

7 Draw up a list of reasons *why* the Good Samaritan might have done what he did for the injured man.

Homework

A Find five examples of human rights abuses in the world today. For one of these find a newspaper story which illustrates it.

or

B Write down three reasons why human rights in other countries should be our concern and three reasons why this might be none of our business.

Freedom and Justice

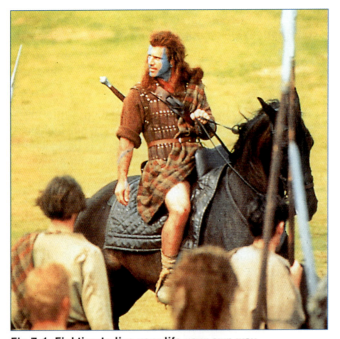

Fig 7.1 Fighting to live your life your own way

They'll never take our freedom!

One basic right is freedom. Freedom can take many forms:

- freedom of movement in your own country and around the world

- freedom to think and believe what you want and to express your thoughts and beliefs

- freedom from pain and suffering

- freedom to choose your own government and so preserve your own way of life (self-determination)

- freedom from slavery and ill-treatment.

DISCUSSION POINT

Why is freedom important?

Like it or leave it

Often people are denied basic freedoms such as these. For example, in Israel, Palestinians say that they are not allowed free access to what they think is their own land. They see Israel as an occupying force and complain bitterly about their treatment:

'When the soldiers come to arrest you ... they call you: "Simon, get up we have come for you", they know all the names ... They get the handcuffs on you and they beat you while they rush you down the hill to the car. And again in the car they beat you.'

Some Israelis respond:

'It's very simple ... this is our country. We have nowhere else to go. Palestinians have more than twenty other Arab countries to choose from. If they don't like it here they should go.'

Both quoted in Bettina Selby: Like Water in a Dry Land

Israelis argue that Israel is their homeland and that it always has been. Their position is that they were forced out of it and so are only reclaiming what is rightfully theirs.

Speaking your mind

During 1998, Amnesty International tried to help more than 5000 people around the world who were imprisoned for their beliefs. Amnesty also produced a 150-page report on human rights abuses – from torture to racial harassment – in the USA, the 'Land of the Free'. Amnesty opposes the imprisonment of anyone who has not supported or used violence. It argues that expressing your beliefs should never be punished.

DISCUSSION POINT

Should people be imprisoned for their beliefs?

Fig 7.2 Whose land is it?

Ruling yourself

The tangled mess of the former Yugoslavia shows the difficulties which can arise when leaders choose to ignore the international community. Slobadan Milosevic, the former leader of Serbia, has been accused of 'crimes against humanity'.

'Ethnic cleansing' has been carried out. This can mean either removing people from your land or pushing people out of their own, depending upon your viewpoint. Serbs have fled from Kosovo, while Albanians are fleeing Serbia into Kosovo. All fear human rights abuses if they stay where they are.

Amnesty reports that Dr Flora Brovina was sentenced to 12 years imprisonment for 'supplying medicines and treating wounded soldiers'. NATO has backed the Kosovars' claim to self-determination. Serbia says that NATO is interfering in Serbia's own internal business.

In 1999, people in East Timor voted for independence. Indonesian-backed soldiers carried out acts of brutality against the civilian population. By the time the UN was able to go in and to try to put things right, many people had been killed.

DISCUSSION POINT

Does the International community have the right to become involved in a country's business?

Justice for all

Justice means fair treatment no matter who, what or where you are. Everyone, for example, has the right to a fair trial. For a fair trial, judges have to look at the evidence – not judge the person.

Everyone also has the right to expect to be treated in humane ways. If they are not, then their leaders can be brought to trial. It is only within the last few years that international justice has really begun to respond to world problems – for example, by bringing to trial those responsible for atrocities in Rwanda, where many people were killed because of their membership of a particular tribal group.

Justice might also involve the right to privacy – though what if respecting your privacy was dangerous? For example, should our use of the Internet be private – even if we are using it to commit crimes?

Justice might also mean the right to an education – though who decides what you should learn?

Satisfying desires

Plato (c.428–347 BC) said that an unjust person (or government) was one where 'the appetite' was not 'checked' by the 'will'. By this, he meant that justice happens when we realise that our wants can never be fully satisfied – so we should hold back and be reasonable. Where there is injustice, it is caused by people thinking that they can do anything to get what they want.

The Buddha, too, said that all of life's suffering is caused by desire which can never be satisfied. An unjust person is one who tries to satisfy their desires, no matter what that does to others. Both Plato and the Buddha believed that justice brings its own rewards, because it 'really satisfies'. A just person will be a contented one.

Fig 7.3 Where now for the world's refugees?

Focus ▸ Justice

In **Buddhism** justice is a matter of cause and effect. Two ideas are important:

- **Hiri** – this is a sense of shame at having done something wrong, though Buddhists don't like to dwell on misdeeds. They prefer to move on in a positive way.

- **Ottapa** – this means taking the consequences of actions into account.

Buddhist believe that justice is acting in a way which is **mindful** of others. **Selfishness** is the greatest wrong. Injustice results in bad karma for the person who acts badly, and makes life more difficult for others. Acting unjustly sets up a karmic pattern which will have negative results for the re-birth of the person who is doing wrong. Buddhists believe that a ruler should behave justly, and that he cannot rule well until he rules himself.

> Buddhism teaches that we are all potential Buddhas ... By virtue of this common potential for enlightenment, all individuals are worthy of respect, and justice therefore demands that the rights of each individual must be protected.
>
> Damien Keown: A Short Introduction to Buddhism

During the Vietnam war, many Buddhist monks publicly burned themselves to death in protest against the killing of innocent civilians. This shows the importance of justice in Buddhism.

Fig 7.4 Buddhist monk makes a point about justice

Sikhs also believe that a ruler must behave justly:

> A King remains installed on the throne by virtue of his good qualities alone.
>
> Adi Granth 992

One of the first acts of Guru Nanak was to get rid of the Hindu caste system among his followers. This had resulted in injustice for some, because they were low-caste. He encouraged all Sikhs to worship and eat together – no matter what caste they were – because all are of equal value in the sight of God. All should be treated fairly. Power doesn't come from being a king, but from ruling wisely.

> What do I gain if you give me a Kingdom? Worthless the glory it brings. Why should the beggar be humbled or taunted; why should he suffer contempt?
>
> Namdev

Sikhs also believe that injustice comes when you put yourself before anyone else. In trying to satisfy your own desires, you will be in conflict with others. Once you reject your own selfishness you will act justly:

> [Selfishness] is the fatal disease of the Soul.
>
> Guru Nanak

Muslims should act justly because, by doing so, they behave towards others as Allah behaves towards them.

> O you who believe, stand out firmly for Allah as just witnesses; and let not the enmity or hatred of others make you avoid justice. Be just: that is nearer to piety; and fear Allah. Verily, Allah is well-acquainted with what you do.
>
> Surah 5:8

The **Qur'an** often calls justice **balance** (Surah 57:25). By this, it means that justice is like a set of scales where good and evil are weighed up and a decision is reached. Islam teaches that Allah is both compassionate and vengeful, and that as well as rewarding he will also punish where it is required. When trying to understand the Qur'an, Muslims will sometimes use **Ijtihad**. This means trying to balance out Islamic teaching so as to do the right thing. For example, the Qur'an teaches that thieves should have their hand cut off (Surah 5:38), but during a famine, Caliph Umar suspended this rule so as to show compassion. Muslims also believe that kindness is its own reward:

> Is there any reward for kindness other than kindness?
>
> Surah 55:60

Activities

Text Questions

1 Write down two 'forms' of freedom.

2 Why do many Palestinians complain about their treatment by Israelis?

3 How do some Israelis reply?

4 Which country was the subject of an Amnesty International report in 1998?

5 Why might some people be surprised by this?

6 Why was Dr Flora Brovina imprisoned?

7 Give two reasons why Serbia might not be happy about NATO bombing.

8 Why might a government want to check your use of the Internet?

9 What did Plato say was the cause of injustice?

10 What do Buddhists believe that a ruler must be before he can rule justly?

11 What did Guru Nanak say about selfishness?

12 What might a Muslim mean by saying that justice is like a set of scales?

Discussion Points

● What kinds of freedom do you think are the most important?

● What restrictions should there be on people's beliefs or movements?

● When do you think people are likely to be punished for their beliefs?

● What do you think is meant by 'crimes against humanity'?

● Should leaders of countries be responsible for the actions of their country?

● What should be considered private?

● How might being just bring contentment?

● What are the responsibilities of a ruler?

Find Out About

● The Palestine–Israel conflict

● The situation in East Timor

● Trials for 'crimes against humanity'

● Arguments for and against the right to privacy

● Search the web under the heading **Freedom**. Find out what this word means to different people.

Tasks

1 Draw up your own 'Charter of Freedom'. Explain what freedoms you think people should have and why they should have them. Perhaps you should think about putting them in order of priority. Doing this will help your group to discuss the issues involved.

2 Following your research into the Palestine–Israel situation, write an imaginary dialogue between Nadim and Leah:

Nadim is a Palestinian Arab who now lives in the Gaza strip. He wants to know why he cannot move freely around his own country.

Leah is an Israeli who believes in the right of Jews to call Israel their homeland.

3 Split into groups and act out the following role play.

Bananaland is a small island in the Pacific Ocean which is split into two equal geographical areas, East and West. East Bananaland's population is around 200, and West Bananaland's is 2000. The East is Muslim and the West Christian. The East has vast mineral deposits and stunning scenery which is good for tourism. The West has neither but has the economic expertise to make use of it. There is one government which governs both East and West. It sits in the West's capital and is made up of 80% Westerners and 20% Easterners. Even in the East, Westerners living there have the best jobs and the best lifestyles. Most Easterners are poor.

In recent elections, Easterners have voted for independence from the West. The West responded to this by moving soldiers into the East to maintain its control. The East has appealed to the United Nations for help. Meanwhile Easterners have vowed to carry out terrorist attacks in the West.

Round the table in New York three people are gathered: the leader of Bananaland's government, the leader of the East Bananaland Independence Movement, and the Secretary General of the United Nations. How do you resolve the conflict before violence gets out of control?

Homework

A Write three reasons why NATO should be involved in Kosovo and three reasons why it should not.

or

B If you became British Prime Minister tomorrow what five things would you do to make Britain a more just society? Write them down and say what effects you think your actions would have.

Equality and Punishment

A fair go for all

Martin Luther King once said:

> I have a dream ... that one day my two little children will be judged, not by the colour of their skin, but by the contents of their character ... I have a dream ... that black men and white men, Jews and Gentiles, Protestants and Catholics will all join together ...

Has this dream come true today? Is it ever likely to? While some people say that everyone should be treated equally – no matter what their circumstances – others say that this won't ever happen. Human nature won't allow it. In the twenty-first century it is still claimed that equality for all isn't here yet.

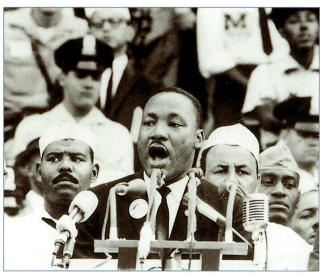

Fig 8.1 Has Martin's dream come true?

Equal rights

The UN declaration begins by stressing the equality of all. But discrimination still happens, based on:

- colour or racial group – in Britain it is claimed that you are far more likely to be picked up by the Police if you are 'non-white'. The case of Stephen Lawrence led many people to look more closely at the treatment of race in the UK. In the USA, most death row prisoners are black. In Australia, many believe that the treatment of Aboriginal people is poor, though since 1970 the Australian government has been returning land to aborigines – but keeping control over mineral rights on that land.

- religion or beliefs – in many countries, certain jobs and privileges are only open to those who have certain beliefs. Catholics in Northern Ireland have long claimed that their career opportunities are far fewer than their Protestant countrymen. The 'job' of British Monarch is still closed to Roman Catholics.

- gender – there still seems to be a wide gap between the rights of men and women. Even in a country like the UK where we have a Queen and have had a woman as Prime Minister, the situation for women generally doesn't seem to have improved greatly. In the developed world, women are often less likely to achieve high positions at work – and many still juggle a career with being a housewife and a mother. In the developing world, much of the back-breaking work is done by women – unpaid. Again, this might be in addition to keeping a home and raising children.

- social status – in many countries there are still examples of discrimination based on social class. In some countries this is based on occupation, in others – like India – on caste distinctions. Here in Britain, many say that the top jobs in society will always go to those from 'higher classes' – especially those who have been to the 'top' public schools.

- disability and age – disabled people regularly complain of unfair treatment despite strict laws in Britain to prevent this. Also, many people claim that when you get to a certain age you are treated differently. In some jobs, for example, you might be considered over the hill by the time you are 30!

DISCUSSION POINT

What examples of discrimination do you know of?

Fig 8.2 **Some are more equal than others**

Political prisoners

All over the world there are 'prisoners of conscience'. These are people who are imprisoned because of their beliefs – beliefs which conflict with the ideas or actions of a government. Often such political prisoners suffer badly. They may be tortured or physically mistreated. They often have no contact with anyone outside. Sometimes they 'disappear' and are never heard of again. In the former Soviet Union there were prison camps known as Gulags. Many people were sent to these harsh Siberian camps because of their beliefs. Many never returned. France recently refused to send a former member of MI6 back to Britain because it believes the crime the British government has accused him of is a political crime.

DISCUSSION POINT

What do you think a 'political crime' might be?

Crime and punishment

When people commit crimes, most of us agree that they should be punished. Most agree that the punishment should fit the crime. The aims of punishment are:

- to keep the person off the streets so that they don't commit the crime again

- to set an example, so that others think twice about doing the same thing. In other words, punishment acts as a deterrent.

Punishments for crimes vary around the world. Human rights activists try to ensure that punishments are fair and reasonable. They argue that any punishment should also involve *rehabilitation*. This means that, while being punished, criminals should also be educated so that they learn what was wrong with their crime. Perhaps then they won't do it again when they are released. However, in some countries rehabilitation isn't possible because of capital punishment.

An eye for an eye

Capital punishment means execution. It is almost always only for crimes which involve killing. It still exists in many countries, including most states of the USA. In the USA in 1997, there were 3222 prisoners waiting for execution. Between 30 to 60 prisoners are executed each year. There are a variety of methods used and there are disagreements about how much the person suffers during their execution. All major human rights organisations oppose capital punishment because:

- There is no room for error. If you execute someone and later discover new evidence which proves their innocence, you can't bring them back.

- It doesn't work as a deterrent. Countries with capital punishment have the same amount of crime as countries without it.

- It gives the wrong message. Executing someone is a strange way to show that killing is wrong.

However, many people think that capital punishment is a good idea in some cases. They think:

- it is the best way to 'repay' murder

- the person will never commit such a crime again

- the person doesn't have to be kept in prison for life, which is costly

- it makes people think twice about committing crime.

DISCUSSION POINT

What do you think of capital punishment?

Fig 8.3 **The right response to crime?**

The **Old Testament or Torah** has many examples of support for capital punishment:

> Eye for eye, tooth for tooth, hand for hand, foot for foot, burn for burn, wound for wound.

Exodus 21:24–25

Many **Christians** use this as the basis for supporting capital punishment – that God is just and believes that punishments should reflect the crime (see also Genesis 9:6). There are many situations where capital punishment is allowed in the Old Testament:

> Anyone who curses his father or mother should be put to death.

Leviticus 20:9

The death penalty is also allowed for activities such as adultery. However, punishment for murder is not straightforward:

> If a man takes a stick and beats his slave – and the slave dies on the spot, the man is to be punished. But if the slave does not die for a day or two, the master is not to be punished.

Exodus 20:20–21

Many Christians feel that the Old Testament's teaching on punishment belongs to the time it was written. The original laws were given to a people who were wandering in the desert – without many rules of their own. Because of this, the laws were very strict.

Jesus questions the death penalty when he rescues a woman who is about to be stoned to death for adultery. He is also quite clear about Old Testament teaching:

> You have heard it said, 'An eye for an eye, tooth for tooth.' But now I tell you: do not take revenge on someone who wrongs you. If anyone slaps you on the right cheek, let him slap your left cheek too.

Matthew 5:38

Jesus seems to be saying that the *constructive* response to wrongdoing is **forgiveness**, not revenge. Even at his own death, he doesn't curse those who have killed him but forgives them (see Luke 23:34).

Many **Muslims** believe that capital punishment is right:

> And if you punish your enemy, then punish them with the like of that which you were afflicted.

Surah 16:126

This is used to support the 'eye for an eye' principle. However, this passage goes on to say:

> But if you endure patiently, truly, it is better for the patient.

Surah 16:126

Muslims believe that **mercy** is an important idea. In most Muslim countries where the death penalty still exists, relatives of the murdered person can save the murderer from execution. Muslims should show as much **forgiveness** to others as Allah shows to them. This could be understood as total forgiveness because Allah is all-forgiving.

> Let them pardon and forgive. Do you not like Allah to pardon you? Allah is forgiving, merciful.

Surah 22:24

The right response to evil is, according to the Qur'an, the same principle as 'turning the other cheek':

> Repel evil with that which is better.

Surah 23:96

Amnesty International is a non-religious organisation. It began in 1961 in response to 'forgotten prisoners'. One of its main ideas is to:

> Abolish the death penalty, torture and other cruel, inhuman or degrading treatment of prisoners.

It argues that the death penalty is responding to violence with violence, and that such a response will never work.

Most non-religious groups argue that capital punishment is wrong because it deals only with the **symptoms** of crime and not the **causes**. The solution is to create a society where no-one feels the need to kill, and to rehabilitate those who do. Prison should be used as a way to rehabilitate the offender as well as protect society from further harm. Murdering murderers is not seen as a sensible option.

Activities

Text Questions

1 What was Martin Luther King's 'dream'?

2 In Australia, which group of people's treatment may be 'poor'?

3 Which 'job' in the UK is still 'closed to Roman Catholics'?

4 Why do many women in the developing world have a difficult life?

5 According to some people who gets the top jobs in Britain?

6 What is a prisoner of conscience?

7 State two of the aims of punishment.

8 What aim of punishment is often stressed by human rights activists?

9 Give two reasons why human rights organisations oppose capital punishment.

10 Give two reasons in support of capital punishment.

11 How might a Christian support capital punishment?

12 How might a Christian oppose capital punishment?

13 What do Muslims mean by 'mercy'?

14 Why does Amnesty International oppose capital punishment?

Discussion Points

● Has Martin Luther King's dream come true? What still needs to be done?

● Why do you think most death row prisoners in the USA are 'non-white'?

● Should women receive the same rights as men?

● Is Britain still a society where social class matters?

● Should a government have the right to imprison people who speak or act against it?

● Is capital punishment no worse than life imprisonment?

● Should capital punishment still exist?

● Should a Christian support capital punishment?

● Is it useless or wrong to respond to violence with violence?

● What is the most important function of punishment?

Find Out About

● The Stephen Lawrence case

● The Northern Ireland situation

● How disabled people are treated in the UK today

● Prisoners of conscience in the world today, how they are treated and how people try to help

● How capital punishment is carried out today

● The work of Amnesty International

● Search the web under the heading **Martin Luther King**. Find out about his beliefs.

Tasks

1 Design and make your own information leaflet: 'The rights of Aboriginal peoples in Australia'.

2 Carry out a class debate on the following topic: 'A woman's place is in the kitchen'.

3 Following your research into Amnesty International, write a letter to a prisoner of conscience.

4 Write a short speech supporting capital punishment.

5 Listen to the speeches of others in the class. Write your own response to one of them.

6 You are on death row, and have been for a year. During that time you have become a follower of a world faith. You are due to be executed in the next few days. You are visited by your Priest/Imam/ Rabbi or other religious leader. Write the discussion which takes place.

7 Create your own information poster on Amnesty International.

Homework

A Find an example of discrimination from a newspaper. Write the story in your own words.

or

B Imagine you are a religious person. You have been asked to write a letter to a prisoner on death row, explaining why your faith supports the death penalty. Write a one-page letter outlining your views.

Powerful Responses

Fig 9.1 Fidel Castro – a dictator?

Power and authority

Human rights abuses by governments are particularly serious. Governments have the responsibility of looking after the interests of people who live in their land.

Modern governments take many forms:

- *Dictatorships* – here a single ruler has complete control. This often follows a military coup. Dictators do not need to take anyone else's wishes into account and base all their decisions on their own beliefs. Dictators usually choose who to hand power on to.

- *Single Party States* – some countries are run by a political party which allows little or no opposition. These States follow 'the Party line'. They usually keep power within their own 'ranks' and pass it on only to members of their own party.

- *Monarchies* – royal families still rule some countries. They make their decisions based on what they think is right. They pass on power to members of their own families. In the UK our Monarchy has only limited powers. Its duties are mostly ceremonial and symbolic.

- *Democracies* – here governments are elected regularly. They are supposed to make decisions based on 'the common good'. In a true democracy, everyone in the country above a certain age has the right to vote.

DISCUSSION POINT

What are the advantages and disadvantages of these forms of government?

Conflicts of interests

Abuses of human rights often happen when a country has to balance the needs of a few people against the needs of many. Governments should protect the majority, but not necessarily at the expense of minorities. Also, sometimes power simply corrupts people, allowing them to carry out wrong acts in the name of 'national interests'.

DISCUSSION POINT

Do you think that 'power corrupts'?

Comfortable compassion?

Some people think that human rights organisations do good work, others argue that it is too easy to criticise what you don't understand. Perhaps governments of the world should be allowed to do as they please, because only they properly understand the situation in their own country.

Perhaps too, human rights organisations are just another example of the rich, powerful and comfortable developed world telling the developing world how to live. Perhaps we should only concern ourselves with our own government, not with countries whose problems we may not understand.

DISCUSSION POINT

Should a government be allowed to do 'as it pleases'?

Responding to human rights abuses

Karl Adolf Eichmann was a Nazi Officer who was responsible for the deaths of many Jews during the holocaust. In 1960 he was taken from Argentina by Israeli secret agents. He was tried in Israel and hanged in 1962. Many Israelis believe that this was an act of justice, in that Eichmann was made to pay for his crimes.

General Augusto Pinochet, the former Chilean leader, was accused of being responsible for the torture and deaths of 3000 people during his leadership. In 1998, Spain tried to extradite him from the UK where he had come for medical treatment. He was held under house arrest in the UK because no-one knew quite what to do. A former world leader hadn't been arrested like this before. The House of Lords and a British court said he should be extradited, but the British government sent him home to Chile on 2 March 2000, saying that he was too ill to stand trial. In Chile he received a hero's welcome.

Fig 9.2 Pinochet: are leaders above the law?

DISCUSSION POINT

Should someone avoid trial because of 'ill-health'?

Nelson Mandela was imprisoned by the South African government in 1962. He was accused of political crimes and of trying to overthrow the South African government. He was finally released in 1990.

Fig 9.3 Burying South Africa's past

In 1994, elections were held in South Africa and he became its President.

He set up a committee known as the Truth and Reconciliation Committee. This group, chaired by Archbishop Desmond Tutu, brought together those who had committed human rights abuses and those who had suffered them. The idea was for those who had suffered abuses to forgive and move on. The aim was for the new South Africa to begin afresh.

The right to a stable world

The UN Declaration of Human Rights includes the following article:

Everyone is entitled to a social and international order in which the rights and freedoms set forth in this Declaration can be fully realised.

Individual human rights are more likely to be safe when society as a whole is balanced and stable. For that to happen, everyone has to be aware of the issues and be able to express reasonable opinions about them. To be able to take part in discussion about world issues, you have to know something about them and to have thought through some of the arguments. It was once said:

For evil to prosper all it takes is for good men to remain silent.

You, the reader, might be a future Prime Minister or world leader. What kind of world will you create?

The **Hindu** teacher **Gandhi** argued that a government should engage in **Swaraj**. This means that it should manage its own affairs. For this to happen, all the members of a society have to be involved in government, by carrying out Swaraj for themselves. This would lead, Gandhi said, to **Purna Swaraj**, or complete self-rule. Everyone plays their part and receives their rewards, no matter who or what they are.

> Swaraj of a people means the sum total of the swaraj of individuals. And such Swaraj comes only from performance by individuals of their duty as citizens.

Gandhi, *Selected Works*, vol VI.

This idea is based on the Hindu concept of **ahimsa**, non-violence. This idea includes allowing everyone the right to behave as they want – provided that doesn't harm anyone else. Gandhi believed that a state was only worthy of support if it acted for the people, and supported **truth**. If it didn't, then in accordance with ahimsa, peaceful protest could win a government over:

> I have always held that social justice, even unto the least and lowliest, is impossible of attainment by force. I have believed that it is possible by proper training of the lowliest by non-violent means to secure the redress of the wrongs suffered by them.

Gandhi, *All Men are Brothers*

For Gandhi, the authority of a state was only to be recognised when it acted justly.

In **Christianity**, the state is considered to be chosen by God. Because of this it should be obeyed.

> Everyone must obey the state authorities, because no authority exists without God's permission, and the existing authorities have been put there by God.

Romans 13:1

What **Paul** means here is that the state is another thing which God uses to care for his people. Earthly rulers are God's way of dealing with daily life – including the opportunity to punish and reward. However, Paul probably doesn't mean that the state should be obeyed whatever it does. Soon after this he adds:

> Be under obligation to no one – the only obligation you have is to love one another. Whoever does this has obeyed the Law.

Romans 13:8

For Christians, the idea is that you should obey the state when it is acting in a fair and just way. Paul shows that the real issue is making sure that you act according to God's law, as set out in the scriptures. When a secular state acts in this way too, it should be supported. When it does not, this is another matter.

Jesus had already made this clear by saying:

> Pay the Emperor what belongs to the Emperor, and pay God what belongs to God.

Mark 12:17

Jesus seems to be saying also that the secular state should be respected, but only when it acts in a way which is respectful to God. In the Book of **Acts**, the apostles refuse to obey the authorities' demands to stop preaching about Jesus. They believe that it is more important to obey God than to obey men (see Acts 5:29).

In **Islam** there is the same tension between the authority of Allah and that of the state:

> Allah [alone] holds control over Heaven and Earth.

Surah 2:107

The state should be obeyed but only when it acts fairly in accordance with the **Qur'an**:

> Co-operate with one another for virtue and heedfulness and do not co-operate with one another for the purpose of vice and aggression. Heed Allah [alone]; Allah is strict with punishment.

Surah 5:2

In particular, when the state acts corruptly it should not be obeyed, because such corruption is not acceptable to Allah:

> Heed God and obey me; do not obey the order of extravagant people who corrupt things on Earth and who do not reform.

Surah 26:150–152

Many Muslim countries, like Pakistan are known as **Islamic States**. These countries base their legal system on the Qur'an.

Muslim authorities believe that it is their duty to put into practice the teachings of the Qur'an. This, they believe, will make society a better place.

Activities

Text Questions

1 What is a dictatorship?

2 What is meant by a democracy?

3 What do some people think power can do to a person?

4 Why might someone disagree with the right of a human rights organisation to protest about abuses in another country?

5 Which country did Eichmann escape to?

6 Why did he run away from Germany?

7 Why was Senator Augusto Pinochet arrested in the UK?

8 What eventually happened to him?

9 How long was Nelson Mandela in prison?

10 What did the Truth and Reconciliation Committee do?

11 What might it take for 'evil to prosper'?

12 When did Gandhi believe a state should be supported?

13 What did Paul teach about obeying the state?

14 When should a Muslim obey the state authorities?

Discussion Points

● Why are human rights abuses carried out by a government so serious?

● Are dictatorships a good or bad way to run a country?

● What are the disadvantages of a democracy?

● What do you think it means to say that 'For evil to prosper, all it takes is for good men to remain silent'? Do you agree?

● Should governments be allowed to solve their own problems?

● Was the treatment of Eichmann fair?

● Should a head of state be above the law?

● Why did Nelson Mandela set up the Truth and Reconciliation committee?

● How can you tell if a state is supporting truth?

● When should Christians oppose the state?

● Does it make sense to base a society on a holy book?

Find Out About

● Modern dictatorships around the world

● The power of different monarchies around the world

● The actions of the Christian Church in Nazi Germany

● Human Rights abuses in Pinochet's Chile

● Apartheid in South Africa

● Gandhi's responses to British rule in India

● Modern Islamic states

● Search the web under the heading **Nelson Mandela**. Find out his story.

Tasks

1 On a world map highlight countries where human rights abuses have taken place in recent years. Now add information about the types of governments found in the countries you highlighted.

2 Carry out a class debate on: 'Britain should give more political power to the Royal Family.'

3 Write a short speech entitled: 'Why everyone should be allowed to vote from the age of 16.'

4 Prepare a display board for your classroom which explains the story of General Pinochet.

5 Write to (or e-mail) Nelson Mandela. What questions would you like to ask?

6 Imagine yourself 20 years older – you have become Prime Minister. What issues would be most important to you? Write your own action plan.

7 Create your own illustrated poster using the quote 'For evil to prosper, all it takes is for good men to remain silent.'

8 You are living in Britain during the time when apartheid in South Africa was in place. Write a newspaper article which explains your beliefs about what your government should do. Explain your own views and how they are based on your understanding of your own beliefs.

Homework

A State two reasons why we should obey the state and give two occasions when we should, perhaps, disobey it.

or

B Find an example of a recent human rights abuse from a newspaper or magazine. Stick it in your workbook and, in your own words, explain how a follower of a world faith might respond.

Do We Really Need to Fight?

War

From ancient texts, such as the Bible, it would seem there have been wars since the beginning of human history. War is always violent with few heroes and many victims. It is always about people being ready to fight, kill and die to get what they want. All wars are different; different countries get involved with different reasons for fighting and different weapons are used. But all wars are the same in one way – violence is used on a massive scale.

Fig 10.1 **Only the uniforms change**

Why do wars happen?

- I want what you've got! Wars are fought for gain.

- We will defend ourselves! Wars are fought to keep a people or country safe.

- We want to be free! Wars are fought to gain freedom.

- Do it my way, or else! Wars are fought in support of an ideology or way of life.

DISCUSSION POINT

Do any of the reasons above justify going to war?

Does it have to be like this?

There have been many attempts through the ages to do away with war altogether. People have seen how cruel, unjust and wasteful war is.

Among Christians, Quakers do not believe in the use of violence in any circumstances. Among the religions of India, Ahimsa or the rejection of violence has a long and honoured tradition. It is especially important to those of the Jain faith who will not take the life of any living thing. During the two great World Wars of the twentieth century, many people refused to go into the army and fight. They were called conscientious objectors.

Most people believe that some situations justify the use of force, but there are many who refuse to accept the way of violence.

DISCUSSION POINT

Can refusing to fight be a way of stopping wars happening?

Fig 10.2 **Gandhi's non-violence**

Two case studies

In 1978 a civil war began in Afghanistan when a Revolutionary Council, backed by the Soviet Union, took over the government by force. The Council wanted an atheistic 'socialist state' modelled on the Soviet Union. The vast majority of the people of Afghanistan were Muslim. Groups took up arms with the aim of restoring Islam to a central place in the life of the country and of driving out the government.

Fig 10.3 Soviet force in Afghanistan

In the 1980s the Soviet Union had about 118,000 troops fighting in Afghanistan. The rebel forces proved determined and, after the Soviet troops withdrew, an Islamic republic was established.

Fig 10.4 The results of 'ethnic cleansing'

The country of Yugoslavia began to break up at the end of the last century. Wars broke out and 'ethnic cleansing' began on a massive scale. Muslims, Catholic Christians and Orthodox Christians had lived peacefully side by side across the country. However, as leaders of the new countries battled for power, attempts were made to create whole areas that were 'ethnically pure'. Millions of people were driven out and many thousands were killed because they were the 'wrong religion'. Ethnic and religious differences were exploited for political ends. Death and destruction resulted and the seeds of hate, which would last far into the future, were spread across the whole region.

DISCUSSION POINT

If one side chooses war, is there any other way the other side can respond except by fighting back?

Any easy answers?

War is violent and destructive, so it is difficult to see how anyone would want to go to war. However, as wars have happened so often and go on happening, perhaps they really are the only way of dealing with certain situations. If war should always be the last resort, perhaps the real political skill is knowing exactly when that last resort has been reached.

DISCUSSION POINT

Do you think wars will always be a part of human life?

Fig 10.5

Focus Prayer

The **Jewish** faith encourages daily prayers which express the hopes and aspirations of believers:

> We bless the Lord who conquers strife, who removes all hatred, and brings harmony to his creation. We praise the God we cannot see, who binds together all His creatures with unseen threads of service and love.

Forms of Prayer The Reform Synagogues of Great Britain

The **Christian** faith is founded on Jesus whose life is told in the **Gospels**. The words of Jesus found in the Gospels are sometimes difficult to reconcile:

> 'You have heard that it was said, "Love your friends and hate your enemies." But now I tell you: pray for those that persecute you, so that you may become children of your Father in heaven.'

Matthew 5:43–44

> 'Do you think I have come to bring peace to the world. No, I did not come to bring peace but a sword. I came to set sons against fathers, daughters against mothers, daughters in law against mothers in law. Your worst enemies will be members of your own family.'

Matthew 10:34–36

Sikhs are called to daily prayer to reflect on the place of God's power in the life of humanity:

> I have no strength to speak and no strength to be silent. I have no strength to ask and no strength to give; I have no strength to live and no strength to die. I have no strength to acquire empire or wealth which trouble the heart. I have no strength to meditate on Thee or reflect on divine knowledge. I have no strength to find the way of escape from the world. He in whose arm there is strength may see what he can do. Nanak, no-one is of greater or lesser strength before God.

From Japuji, the morning prayer

Hinduism teaches that God becomes involved in human affairs at different times in the life of the world, sometimes as a human incarnation or **Avatar**, and sometimes as a God.

> When you, O Indra, harness your chariot there is no greater warrior than you, none equal to you in strength, none, however good his horse, has ever overtaken you. It is Indra who alone gives wealth to the kind and well-disposed man. His heroism is undisputed and he is lord of immense strength. When will you trample on the godless ones who have no gifts to offer, as if upon a coiled snake?

From the Hindu text *Rigveda* (Indra is the Vedic God of battle)

Fig 10.6 Time out from combat for prayer

Activities

Text Questions

`1 Why can we say war has been around for a long time?

2 What is a 'conscientious objector'?

3 What is Ahimsa?

4 The break up of which country led to 'ethnic cleansing'?

5 Which country supported the Revolutionary Council in Afghanistan?

6 What were the three main religions of the people of Yugoslavia?

7 What was the religion of the vast majority of the people in Afghanistan at the time of the civil war?

8 What are the Gospels?

9 What is the Japuji?

10 What is an Avatar?

Discussion Points

● How do you think the various faith teachings would guide people if they found themselves asked to go and fight for their country?

● Which of the faith teachings do you think is most helpful? Which do you find least helpful?

● Is there anything so important to you that it is worth dying for?

● Is there anything so important to you that you might kill for it?

● What do you think about the reasons for going to war given in the examples?

Fig 10.7 Taliban fighters in Afghanistan

Find Out About

● The countries that arose out of the break-up of Yugoslavia

● The result of the 'ethnic cleansing'

● Why the Soviet Union supported the establishment of a socialist state in Afghanistan

● The things that have happened in Afghanistan since it became an Islamic republic

● Find out about a war which is not mentioned in this unit. Write about it saying:
  – where it happened
  – why it started
  – who was involved
  – what the result was

● The last war in which British troops were involved

● Search the web under the heading **United Nations**. Find out how wide the range of the UN's activities are today and say in what ways it contributes to avoiding wars.

Homework

A Imagine a discussion between a pacifist who would never fight whatever the reason and a soldier who feels that, under certain circumstances, it is necessary to fight, kill and perhaps die.

Write a short statement from each one giving the reasons which they might think are most important.

or

B The United Nations was set up after World War Two to continue the work of the League of Nations and enable member countries to deal with international disputes. One of the main aims was to try to prevent international disputes becoming wars. Find out how the United Nations makes decisions and say whether you think it is a good way of dealing with international disputes or not.

or

C You are a BBC television reporter. You are in a country which has just been invaded by a powerful neighbour which wants to install a more friendly government. The invaded country has no real army but wants to resist. Write a 30-second news item, featuring the picture of a captured tank, which tells the viewers that a war will probably be unavoidable.

The Only Way?

What makes people choose war?

Killing, wounding and destroying is a serious business. Wars always involve destruction and death, whatever else they may be about. And they don't just happen. Leaders don't sit down and decide in a friendly way to kill each others' soldiers and citizens, and destroy their cities. No-one seems to want wars, but wars keep on happening. The killing goes on and on, and people suffer. War is a terrible affair and very unpredictable in how it will turn out. So why do so many leaders continue to see war as a way of dealing with the issues they face?

Fig 11.2 Kuwait City on fire

Home and away

Wars can be grouped into two main categories: international wars and civil wars. International wars are fought between two or more countries; civil wars happen when groups within the same country take military action against each other. Wars happen for different reasons:

- Going to war is a sign of strength. It shows you really mean business.

- If the government denies people freedom of speech, imprisons opponents or uses violence to stay in power, what else can people do but take up arms?

- A war can finish things. Negotiations and discussions can go on and on but, in the end, may get nowhere.

- If you don't stand up to a country which threatens force, you finish up by giving in.

- Wars are necessary every so often to let out the natural violence that builds up in people and countries.

Fig 11.1 The results of war

DISCUSSION POINT

Who do you think ought to make the decision for a country to go to war? How should the decision be reached?

DISCUSSION POINT

Do any of the above reasons make sense of decisions to go to war?

As simple as it seems?

In 1990 Saddam Hussein, the dictator of Iraq, invaded the neighbouring oil-rich country of Kuwait. The United Nations sent in a 500,000 strong force. After two months of fighting, Iraq agreed to a provisional ceasefire after their forces had been driven out of Kuwait.

Fig 11.3 Oil fields blaze as Iraqi troops withdraw

It seemed to be a matter of the 'goodies' punishing the 'baddies'. But was it?

Saddam Hussein was shown in the West as a wicked dictator who was manufacturing chemical weapons to use in the Middle East. But Iraq under Hussein had good levels of health and education for the region. Hussein also claimed that Kuwait had been part of Iraq, and had been taken away illegally and turned into a separate country. Although he was seen in the West as a cruel dictator, many in the Middle East saw him as one of the few leaders who would stand up to the USA and not allow it to run the region by supplying money, arms and political support to friendly governments.

DISCUSSION POINT

Which do you think was more important, opposing Iraq's aggression or finding out the true state of affairs in the region?

Is there a bottom line?

It would be much better for everyone concerned if the decision to go to war, for whatever reason, could be made when all the facts were known, after discussion and negotiation had been tried and after ensuring that no innocent people would get hurt. That never happens! It is usually a question of 'if someone's going to start kicking, kick them first before they kick you!' One thing is certain – if you're going to go to war, you want to win, second best is nowhere. So when people think war is a probability, reason and care go out the window. Whoever heard of a polite army winning?

- When countries are at war the information they supply to the world often becomes propaganda.

- When a war becomes likely it becomes harder not easier for negotiations and discussions to take place.

- Wars need preparation and once countries start to prepare, war becomes much more likely.

- Once a country goes to war its forces are committed to winning and the normal rules of life get suspended.

DISCUSSION POINT

Are there any circumstances you can think of which justify starting a war?

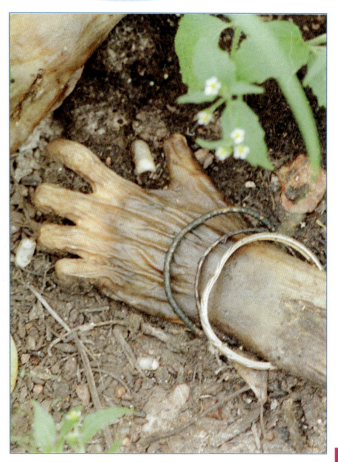

Fig 11.4 This is the reality of war

Focus ▸ War

There can be very few decisions more serious than whether it is right or wrong to wage war. Believers have traditionally turned to their religion when faced with such big decisions.

Buddhists try to dedicate their lives to becoming free of human passions and emotions – to become detached. But they are not supposed to ignore their fellow human beings:

> May I be a protector of the helpless, a guide to those travelling the path, a boat to those wishing to cross over, or a bridge or a raft.
>
> May I be a lamp for those in darkness, a home for the homeless and a servant to the world.

from the Buddhist text Bodhicaryavatara

The **Jain faith** encourages believers to respect life in all its forms. Jains have been known to carry brushes to sweep away any small creatures they might stand on by accident. **Ahimsa**, the rejection of violence, is very important in Jain belief and practice:

> I forgive all living beings, let all living beings forgive me. All in this world are my friends, I have no enemies.
>
> Let the whole universe be blessed. Let all beings engage in one another's well-being.

Jain Scriptures

Hindu prayer frequently dwells on peace and prayers can often be concluded with the word **shanti** (peace):

> May there be peace in heaven, may there be peace in the skies, may there be peace on earth, may there be peace in the waters, may there be peace in the plants, may there be peace in the trees. May we find peace in all the divine powers, may we find peace in the supreme lord. May we all be in peace and may that peace be mine.

The Vedas

The **Sikhs** were persecuted by both Hindu princes and Muslim emperors. For a long time, Sikhs rejected violence but finally, under Guru Gobind Singh, they began to fight to protect themselves and their faith. Sikhs do not believe that God can be persuaded, but they seek God's guidance and rely on God's wisdom and generosity in all aspects of life.

> For success in any task seek first the grace of God. He will grant you success. So says the true teacher and guide. In the company of the holy saints taste the nectar of God's name, the dispeller of doubts, the merciful one. Protect the honour of your follower. Sing the praises of God and then you shall know the unknowable.

Guru Ram Das. Fourth Sikh Guru

Fig 11.5 Sikh ceremonial swords, a reminder of history and duty

Activities

Text Questions

1 Who fights in an international war?

2 Who fights in civil war?

3 How did the West portray Saddam Hussein?

4 What reason did Iraq give for invading Kuwait?

5 Who sent forces to oppose Saddam Hussein?

6 Give three reasons why people go to war.

7 How do wars never start?

8 What do Buddhists try to achieve during their lives?

9 What is the Hindu word for peace?

10 Which Sikh Guru organised the Sikhs to fight to defend their faith?

Discussion Points

● Is there anything you can think of which might happen in Britain that could lead to civil war?

● How would you expect Jain believers to behave if a war broke out around them?

● Can waging war ever be an acceptable way of bringing peace?

● Most religions encourage believers to seek the will of God. Do you think it is possible to know exactly what action God would want taken if war was a possibility?

● Do the quotes in the Focus help in a discussion about when it is right to fight?

Fig 11.6 All his family are dead

Find Out About

● The ways in which Saddam Hussein behaved as a cruel dictator

● The last civil war in England and what it was about

● From history and up to the present, any wars which were caused or fought for religious reasons

● The countries that are involved in civil war at the present time

● Search the web under the heading **Pacifism**. Find out about some arguments put forward concerning non-violence.

Homework

A Read the following list of situations:

● someone laughs at your hairstyle

● someone swears at you or abuses you because of your race

● someone ignores you

● someone steals from you

● the government introduces a law which you feel is both wicked and unjust

● your country is invaded.

Put this list into what you think is the order of seriousness, starting with the most serious and finishing with the least serious. Then write what you think your response would be if these situations arose for you.

or

B You are foreign correspondent for a national newspaper. You are in a country on the edge of civil war. This farmer returns but all his family are dead. Write a short piece of no more than 150 words to go with the picture explaining why civil war would make things worse even for those whose families have already been killed.

In a War, Who Wins? Who Loses?

It is estimated that 30 million civilians died in World War Two, which lasted from 1939–45. In the bombing of Dresden alone 135,000 civilians died in one night. But wars don't only kill. In 1945 there were 12 million refugees without a country. Since 1945, wars have created well over 50 million refugees, and the count is rising. Wars have also led to terrible crimes. Over 6 million Jews were murdered in death camps during World War Two and over 7 million Jews were forced into exile.

Fig 12.1 Concentration camp victims

So, if the price of war is so terrible, why does anyone pay it?

- To achieve any great cause, there always has to be some sacrifice.

- Civilians are not always innocent just because they are not in uniform.

- Everybody dies, so dying for a good cause isn't really such a bad thing.

DISCUSSION POINT

What do you think of the three reasons given above?

So who are the winners?

Fig 12.2 Victorious soldier

The winners in any war obtain power, wealth, resources, financial, religious or political advantage. But to win you needn't actually fight! A great number of civil wars were fought in Africa in the late twentieth century. Often, the rival armies were armed, trained and supported by either the Soviet Union or the USA. These two superpowers could not fight each other without risking an all-out nuclear war, so they tried to extend their political influence by taking sides in what became known as proxy wars – wars fought for them by other countries. It's not a bad way to get what you want, is it? You supply the money, arms, know-how and propaganda and, if you back the winner, you get all you want and none of your people gets hurt.

East Timor

East Timor was a Portuguese colony until 1975. When the Portuguese withdrew, the Indonesian Army invaded and East Timor was annexed to Indonesia. The invasion was declared illegal by the United Nations. The population of East Timor was predominantly Christian and the predominant faith of Indonesia was Islam, but religion was not the reason for the invasion. The Indonesian government wanted East Timor's resources.

A guerrilla opposition to the invaders began, and between 1975 and 1998 it was estimated that over 200,000 people had been killed by the occupying forces out of a population of 700,000.

Peaceful opposition to the occupying forces was led by Bishop Carlos Belo, who received the Nobel Peace Prize for his work in East Timor. A vote on independence was carried out and the Indonesian military withdrew. A United Nations peace-keeping force moved in until the future of the country became clear. As the twenty-first century began, East Timor and Indonesia remained an area of uncertainty and violence.

Fig 12.4 Graves of victims in East Timor

In the end . . .

It has been said that the history of wars is only ever written by the winners. If this is true, then history only ever tells one side of the story – the story of the losers probably never gets told.

Fig 12.5

Fig 12.3 Violence just below the surface in East Timor

Focus ▶ Faith

The **Christian** faith has always preached peace on Earth. This prayer was written by the great Christian saint, Francis of Assisi:

> Let me be an instrument of your peace. Where there is hatred let me sow love; where there is injury, pardon; where there is doubt, faith; where there is despair, hope; where there is darkness, light; where there is sadness, joy.

However, in the Gospels we are told of the time when Jesus went to the temple in Jerusalem, the most holy place, and found people with stalls and tables selling animals for offerings and changing money for foreigners. His reaction was quite aggressive:

> So he made a whip from cords and drove all the animals out of the temple, both the sheep and the cattle; he overturned the tables of the moneychangers and scattered their coins; and he ordered those who sold pigeons, 'Take them out of here! Stop making my Father's house a market place!'

John 2:13–16

The Christian Churches have always had different views on the price of peace. **Quakers** are strict pacifists and will not fight. Violence, they say, cannot lead to peace. But many Christians believe that peace needs to be defended and, sometimes, force may be the only effective response.

The faith of **Islam** has never been completely pacifist, but it does not support the use of violence. The very name Islam comes from the Arabic word **slm** which means peace. The Qur'an lays down clear guidance on the use of force as it does for all aspects of life:

> Fight in the way of God with those who fight with you, but aggress not: God loves not the aggressors.

Surah 2:187

And violence should only be used as little as possible. Even when violence has to be used, it should stop as soon as possible:

> If the enemy inclines towards peace, then you should also incline towards peace.

Surah 8:61

But to fight and perhaps die in the cause of Islam, defending it against those who attack it or try to prevent the faithful from practising their faith, may be the duty of the devout Muslim:

> And those who are slain in the way of God ... He will admit them to Paradise ...

Surah 47:7

For the **Muslim**, the Qur'an is the guide to life. But knowing when and how to apply the teachings of the Qur'an, in all the different situations of life, requires prayer, thought, wisdom and faith.

Fig 12.6 Auschwitz concentration camp: is it possible to pray in such a place of death?

Activities

Text Questions

1 How many civilians died in World War Two?

2 How many Jews were murdered in death camps?

3 Who do they say writes the history of wars?

4 Which superpowers fought the 'proxy wars'?

5 Who 'wins' from wars?

6 Who won the Nobel Peace Prize for his work in East Timor?

7 Who was Francis of Assisi?

8 What did Jesus do when he found people selling things in the temple?

9 What word does Islam come from and what does the word mean?

10 What does the Qur'an instruct Muslims to do if their enemy wants to make peace?

Discussion Points

● Which do you think is more important, peace or justice?

● If Jesus preached peace and forgiveness, why did he drive the dealers out of the temple?

● If it is wrong for Muslims to be aggressors, must they always wait to be attacked before defending themselves?

● If you had lived between 1939 and 1945 in Britain, how would the quotes in the Focus have influenced your thinking about the bombing of enemy civilian targets like Dresden?

Find Out About

● The situation in East Timor and Indonesia

● What happens at 11am on 11 November each year

● How and why the state of Israel was founded after World War Two

● The number of civilians who were killed as a result of wars last year

● Search the web under the heading **Holocaust**. Find out when and how the persecution of Jews in Germany began under Nazism. Do you think, from what you have found, that other countries should have intervened earlier to stop the Nazi persecution?

Homework

A Imagine you were Prime Minister of Britain in 1941. Coventry has just been bombed with massive destruction and loss of civilian lives. What things would you need to consider in deciding whether Britain should, in turn, bomb targets such as enemy cities?

or

B Imagine you are a refugee driven away from your home and family by war. Write what your feelings are about war and those people who make war on civilians.

or

C Imagine someone from Hollywood wanted to make a feature film about the Nazi persecution of the Jews and wanted to use Auschwitz Concentration camp for filming. Write a letter of no more than 150 words explaining why filming for such a picture could never be allowed at the site of the camp.

No Weapons – No Problems?

Making weapons

About 100 years ago 'the war to end all wars' was fought with rifles, artillery, ships, submarines, primitive planes, mines, poison gas and tanks. The slaughter these weapons caused horrified everyone and, for a time, future wars seemed impossible. But today weapons production is a multi-billion pound industry across the world. The cost of a modern combat aircraft can be as much as $2 billion. Think what $2 billion could buy in terms of 'community welfare' spending. Think what $2 billion could do for the poor of a developing country. But making and selling weapons is part of the economy of many countries, including Britain. It is necessary to remember that the industry provides employment and income to a great many people. The wages and profits from the arms industry all go back into society, just like the wages and profits from other industries. And, as everyone knows, while weapons are wanted, somebody will make and sell them.

Fig 13.1 World War One graves

- Weapons are becoming more expensive and more destructive.

- If we don't produce weapons somebody else will.

- Being a really big weapons producer means you can influence and control the kinds of weapons that are available, and make sure things like chemical weapons are never used.

- If you don't produce weapons yourself, what happens when you really need them?

Fig 13.2 Selling the means of death – an armaments fair

DISCUSSION POINT

If you lived in a place with high unemployment and a big weapons manufacturer wanted to set up a factory, what action, if any, would you advise the local people to take?

Bang! We're all dead

The most horrifying weapon developed in the twentieth century was the nuclear bomb. At the beginning of the twenty-first century, nuclear devices and their delivery systems were so powerful that, for the first time in the history of the world, mankind had the capacity to wipe itself completely off the face of the Earth!

Fig 13.3 Atom bomb in Japan

But no-one would use them . . .

Oh yes they would. Nuclear weapons have already been used twice in a war situation. Two nuclear bombs were dropped on Japan in 1945, on Hiroshima and Nagasaki. They were quite small in destructive power, compared to modern nuclear weapons. But they destroyed an area of about 8 square miles, and killed or injured around 200,000 people. It will probably never be known how many people were affected by radiation from the bombs as radiation-related sicknesses continued appearing in people and in new-born infants many years after the bombs were dropped.

DISCUSSION POINT
What do you think were the reasons for deciding to use atomic weapons against Japan?

Why not get rid of them?

Nuclear weapons were at the heart of what became known as the 'Cold War' between the USA and the Soviet Union. These two superpowers clashed politically and war seemed likely. Indeed a third world war seemed to be about to begin many times between 1946 and 1991, when the Soviet Union finally broke up. But no war actually took place. It is thought by many people that there was no war because both sides possessed nuclear weapons and had the ability to deliver them to all parts of each other's country. Any war would have brought about the annihilation of both countries, and perhaps the rest of the world. A violent and dangerous peace? True – but was it a better option than a war which really would end all wars?

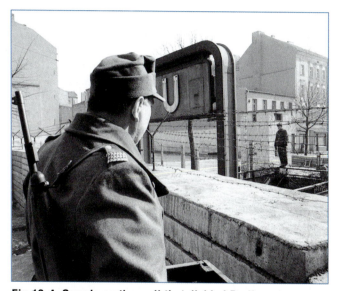

Fig 13.4 Guards on the wall that divided Berlin

DISCUSSION POINT
Are there any circumstances where you think nuclear weapons might be used again?

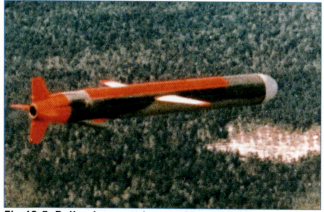

Fig 13.5 Delivering a modern nuclear warhead

Focus · Just war

Christians have evolved a way of dealing with war by working out a **Just War Theory**. This theory shows very well the Western tradition of **faith** combined with **reason**. Military force can never be aggressive and may only be used when all the following conditions apply:

- The damage inflicted by the aggressor is lasting, serious and certain to happen.

- All means other than military force must have been shown to be of no use.

- There must be a real possibility of success.

- The use of military force must not produce any evil greater than the evil being opposed.

This theory was worked out many centuries ago when weapons were quite simple by modern standards. Christians still try to use it but find it difficult in the face of modern weapons manufacture.

Here is part of a letter written in 1845 by Chief Seattle when he was asked by the President of the United States to sell Indian land to the government. He knew that if he refused force would be used against his people and, because they didn't have the weapons to resist, they would lose the land.

How can you buy or sell the sky, the warmth of the land? The idea is strange to us. Every part of this Earth is sacred to my people. Every shining pine needle, every sandy shore, every mist in the dark woods, every clearing is holy in the memory and experience of my people. The white man's dead forget the country of their birth when they go to walk among the stars. Our dead never forget this beautiful Earth. Teach your children what we have taught our children, that the Earth is their mother. Whatever befalls the Earth befalls the sons of Earth. We know the Earth does not belong to man, man belongs to the Earth. This we know, all things are connected. Man did not weave the web of life, he is merely a strand in it. Whatever he does to the web, he does to himself. Even the white man, whose God walks and talks with him as friend to friend, must be part of the destiny of all things. One thing we know, which the white man may one day discover – our God is the same God. You may think you own him as you wish to own the land, but you cannot. He is the God of man and his compassion is equal for the red man and the white. The Earth is precious to Him, and to harm the Earth is to heap contempt on its Creator.

Fig 13.6 North American chiefs meet those who will decide the future

Activities

Text Questions

1 What weapons were used in the war of 1914–18?

2 About how much does a modern combat bomber cost?

3 Which two Japanese cities had nuclear bombs dropped on them in 1945?

4 What was the area of destruction and how many people were killed or injured by the nuclear bombs dropped on Japan?

5 What terrible thing was mankind finally capable of by the beginning of the 21st century?

6 What are the four conditions necessary for a 'Just War' in the Christian tradition?

7 Who wanted to buy land from the native American Indians in 1845?

8 Who set out the native American Indian understanding of owning land?

9 Which two superpowers were involved in the 'cold war'?

Discussion Points

- What, if any, do you see are the moral problems of working in the arms industry?

- What do you think would be the consequences if all British companies involved in weapons production pulled out of the arms industry?

- Could nuclear weapons be used as part of a 'Just War' according to Christian tradition?

Fig 13.7 Helicopter gunship

- Which do you think is likely to be better in controlling the use and spread of weapons, the 'faith and reason' tradition of Western countries or the 'sacred Earth' tradition as expressed by Chief Seattle?

Find Out About

- The British companies that are involved in arms manufacture, what they make and how many people they employ

- What different faiths say about the business of manufacture and sale of non-nuclear weapons

- The countries, today, that are known to possess nuclear weapons

- What different faiths say about the morality of having and possibly using nuclear weapons

- Search the web under the heading **CND (Campaign for Nuclear Disarmament)**. Find out about the development of the atom bomb and its first use.

Homework

A Write out what you think are sensible reasons for and against British companies being involved in making and selling arms.

or

B Choose either the 'just war' tradition or the 'sacred Earth' tradition and write an argument for Britain's withdrawal from arms manufacture.

or

C You are an investigative journalist who has found that helicopter gunships built and exported by a British firm are being used by a government with an appalling human rights record against their own people to crush opposition. Write an article of no more than 200 words to go with this picture of why British companies should not sell arms to regimes with bad human rights records.

It's Good to Belong

Being British

There are different views on Britishness.

- There is no such thing as being British, we are just different people living together in Britain.

- If you are born in Britain, you're British whatever your faith or culture

- People move about the world so much these days labels like British, European or African have become meaningless.

- Being British means living and working with others for the good of all the people who live in Britain.

- Being British is a way of life with traditions and values based in British history that must be passed on.

Fig 14.1 Smile please – you're all in this

DISCUSSION POINT

Can you find a useful and meaningful way of describing what it is to be British?

People have always wanted to belong, to be part of a group, tribe or society, expressing who they are by doing things together. People have shared language, beliefs, laws, ways of organising leadership and even ways of thinking. All of these things, taken together as a way of living, can be called culture.

When European explorers and armies began to set out across the globe in the sixteenth century they took their Western culture with them and often set about destroying or converting the cultures they found in Africa, Asia and the Americas. Britain was the most successful colonising country and acquired the largest empire the world has seen. A twentieth-century result of all this empire building was that Britain became a multi-cultural and multi-faith society. Britain entered the twenty-first century realising that a respect for diversity was essential for the good of society. But it was also clear that the many different cultural and faith traditions in Britain could lead to inter-communal disputes and even violence. The people of Britain found that one of the great tasks of the twenty-first century, not only for Britain and Europe but for the world, was ensuring that the meeting and mixing of cultures and faiths should be peaceful and a source of progress rather than a source of struggle and mistrust. Everybody now belongs to the Global Village.

DISCUSSION POINT

In what ways is it true to say that the world is growing smaller?

The enemy within!

Ignorance in a multi-cultural, multi-faith society can be a breeding ground for fear and hatred, and can lead to people becoming enemies instead of allies. Groups can look to protect their own interests even if this hurts the common good. But cultures take many centuries to develop and cannot be quickly or easily understood by those outside the culture. And even when something is known, it may not be easy to understand or accept.

To take a specific example, the food rules of many cultures arise from religious beliefs:

- Jews believe that God gave Moses, the greatest Jewish prophet, rules to live by. Certain animals were unclean and could not be eaten.

- Muslims accept the Jewish tradition of prophets and they believe that the last and greatest prophet was Muhammad. They also believe that God gave rules for people to live by which included food laws. Muhammad received these rules and they were written down as the Qur'an.

- Buddhists or Jains believe that no animal should be killed and, therefore, most are vegetarian.

- Hindu practices vary. Some are vegetarian out of respect for all animal life and others are not, but to all Hindus the cow is a sacred animal and no Hindu can eat beef.

- Christians have no forbidden foods. What each Christian eats is a matter of choice, but some Christians do not eat meat on certain holy days.

Given that there are many faith rules, like the food laws of different religions, it is plain to see how, in a multi-cultural, multi-faith society, offence can easily be given.

Fig 14.3

How can we all belong?

Differences can lead to ways of showing tolerance and understanding. The Sikhs lived among Hindus, Muslims and Jains. They developed a tradition that the Gurdwara should not only be a place of worship, but a place of hospitality for anyone in need. After worship, a meal is prepared but it is always a vegetarian meal. Sikhs are not required to be vegetarians but out of tolerance and hospitality they choose to be vegetarian in the Gurdwara.

Fig 14.2 Kosher butcher French style

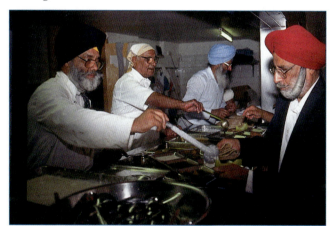

Fig 14.4 Gurdwara meal after worship

DISCUSSION POINT

Do different cultural or faith groups' ways of living help or harm a society?

DISCUSSION POINT

What are the advantages of allowing different faiths to operate side by side in a society and what problems could arise when different faiths exist closely together?

Focus · The common good ····················

Religious faith is almost always a shared faith – which is why faith is often an important part of culture. The **common good**, which arises out of recognising the importance and value of others, is a feature of many religious faiths.

A guru asked his followers how they could tell when night had ended and day begun.

One said, 'When you can see an animal in the distance and can tell whether it is a cow or a horse.'

'No,' said the guru.

'When you look at a tree in the distance and can tell if it is a neem tree or a mango tree.'

'Wrong again,' said the guru.

'Well then, what is it?' said the followers.

'When you look in the face of any man and recognise your brother in him. When you look in the face of any woman and recognise your sister in her. If you cannot do this, no matter what time it is by the sun, it is still night for you.'

Anthony de Mello, *The Prayer of the Frog*

We say in Africa 'a person is a person through other persons'. We are bound together in a delicate network of interdependence. We believe in ubuntu – my humanity is caught up in your humanity. Ubuntu speaks of generosity, of compassion, of hospitality, of sharing. I am, because you are.

Bishop Desmond Tutu, *The Cardiff Justice and Peace newsletter*

The 'common good' may seem straightforward – each helping others for the good of all. But when cultures and faith traditions clash the common good can seem distant from what people *actually* do to each other.

Nowhere did the common good seem so hard to achieve as in Northern Ireland, where violence and mistrust between the Catholic Christian Republicans and the Protestant Christian Unionists seemed to become a way of life during the twentieth century. But even after a terrible history the common good was eventually recognised. The Presbyterian Church, the largest Protestant Christian Church in Northern Ireland, distributed a document to be read out in all its churches when a peace agreement seemed to be possible as the twentieth century closed and a new century began. It contained the following passages:

'Jesus Christ loves all the people of this island regardless of their political preferences or backgrounds ... Since [the Kingdom of God] ... is not restricted to any national boundaries or cultural identities, our political allegiances may never make the first claim on our hearts.'

Fig 14.5 Trying to make peace in Northern Ireland

Activities

Text Questions

1 What is culture?

2 What did Europeans do to the cultures they found when they built their empires?

3 Why did Britain become such a multi-cultural, multi-faith society?

4 Why is ignorance an enemy of a multi-cultural, multi-faith society?

5 Why are Jews not allowed to eat certain meats?

6 What animal is sacred to Hindus?

7 What food laws do Christians have?

8 How do Sikhs show tolerance of other people's beliefs?

9 When is it day according to the guru in *The Prayer of the Frog*?

10 Which two Christian denominations mistrusted each other in Northern Ireland?

Discussion Points

● Why do you think Europeans felt their culture was better than those they found in Africa, Asia and America? Do you think they were right or wrong in the way they thought?

● How important to British society is the common good?

● How important is it for different cultures to be able to keep their beliefs, values and traditions in British society?

● What might be the problems for a society, arising out of the different faith traditions, such as food laws.

Fig 14.6 Multi-faith pilgrimage

● The Focus quotes are all from Christians who come from different cultures. Anthony de Mello came from India, Bishop Tutu from South Africa and the last quote is from Northern Ireland. Is belonging to a particular faith tradition a help or a problem in creating the common good?

Find Out About

● The countries that were once part of the British Empire

● The number of different faith communities that have places of worship in the city where you live, or the city nearest to you

● Other religious food laws

● The causes of violence and mistrust in Northern Ireland

● Search the web under the heading **Culture**. Find information on two countries which you think have different cultures. Write a comparison showing how the countries are different.

Homework

A Imagine that you are going to open a restaurant in an area of Britain with mixed cultures and faith traditions. What foods would you serve and how would you try to make sure customers from all cultural backgrounds felt comfortable with the menu?

or

B What do you think are the problems and advantages to a society of having citizens belonging to many different cultures and faiths?

or

C You are a foreign correspondent for an Indian daily newspaper. Write a 250-word article to go with the picture of a multi-faith pilgrimage saying what needs to be done in Britain today to promote good race relations.

Everyone's Different

Where did we all come from?

Charles Darwin was a scientist who travelled across the world on the survey ship Beagle from 1831–36. From the observations and notes he made he wrote a book, *Origin of Species*. This work led to a theory of evolution which held that all life evolved from some common origin and that all differences could be accounted for by the laws of nature.

Fig 15.1 Charles Darwin

Darwin's theory led many scientists and others to the modern belief that God is not necessary to explain the world and everything in it. Darwin believed that the great variety of life forms present in the animal and plant world was due to the different conditions, such as habitat and weather, in which they had evolved.

Fig 15.2 One way of living . . .

Fig 15.3 . . . and another

DISCUSSION POINT

What do you think about the theory that people, and all other living things, evolved and were not created by God?

Race isn't about running!

The term 'race' is often used as a way of classifying people, but it isn't really very good at the job. 'Race' classifications have usually centred around a number of main groups: European, East Asian, Native American, Sub-Saharan African and Oceanic. The trouble is it can leave out whole groups of peoples who don't fit, such as the peoples of the Indian sub-continent whose physical characteristics vary very widely.

The term can also be stretched to include people who look very different. 'European' includes the very fair people from the far north and the darker people from the Mediterranean. But perhaps the biggest problem with 'race' is that it has often been used to express a supposed inferiority. For instance, skin colour can tell us nothing about intelligence, honesty or ability but it has been used for victimising dark-skinned peoples.

History is full of examples of one group behaving as if other physically different groups were inferior.

And this still happens today.

DISCUSSION POINT

Look at the pictures below. Have a go at classifying the people in the pictures by 'race'. Their country of origin is given on page 63.
What is your opinion of the value of classifying people by 'race'?

Fig 15.6 Number 3

Fig 15.4 Number 1

Fig 15.7 Number 4

Fig 15.5 Number 2

Fig 15.8 Number 5

Focus ▸ God's creatures

Most religions see all humanity as God's creation and require believers to honour God by honouring all of creation, especially fellow human beings.

The **Baha'i faith** was founded by Abdul Baha (also known as Baha' Allah) in 1844 and it first grew in Iraq and Iran. Abdul Baha saw himself as the latest prophet in a long line of divine revelation.

> Clean your eyes so that you see no-one as different from yourselves. See no strangers; rather see all as friends, for love and unity are hard to come by when all you can see are differences. In this new and wonderful age the holy writings say that we must be at one with every people.

Abdul Baha

Taoism is part of Chinese religion and culture. The **Tao** is the source from which all else springs and all life forms, including humans, seek to return to the Tao for renewal. Everything has a common origin in the Tao.

> As we glance over the Taoist books of discipline all say that those who seek immortality must set their minds on gaining merit and doing good works. Their hearts must be kind to all things. They must treat others as they treat themselves and give kind treatment even to insects. They must share the gladness of others and pity their suffering, help those in trouble and give to the poor. Their hands must never injure life and their mouths never speak evil.

P'ao-P'u Tzu, a famous Taoist teacher

The following short story is an illustration of the **Buddhist** way of dealing with other people:

> There are three kinds of person; one is like a drought, one like local rain and one like rain that falls everywhere.
>
> The person like a drought gives nothing to anyone, no food or drink, no clothing or help or shelter. Such a person gives nothing to the important or the lowly. Such a person is like a drought.
>
> The person like a local rainfall gives only to those nearby who are like him.
>
> The one who is like rain everywhere helps all, the important and the lowly, giving food, help, shelter as they are needed. In this way a person rains everywhere.

Itivuttaka

Hinduism teaches the common origin of all things – the **Ultimate Reality** – everything springs from this cosmic centre so all things, even though different, are ultimately the same.

> As a thousand sparks spring from a fire blazing, each one looking like the other, so from the Imperishable all things spring forth and return to him.

Mundaka Upanishad (the Upanishads are ancient Hindu texts written in Sanskrit)

Fig 15.9 A fire blazing

Activities

Text Questions

1 Who was Darwin?

2 What book did he write?

3 What theory came from his work?

4 Using the term 'race' is a way of doing what?

5 What are some of the main classifications using 'race'?

6 What has 'race' often been used to do?

7 Who founded the Baha'i faith and when and where did this happen?

8 In which country did Taoism develop?

9 The Itivuttaka is writing from which faith?

10 What does Hinduism see as the common origin of all things?

Discussion Points

● Do you think modern scientific thought and discoveries have made the idea of God as creator harder for people to believe in or can belief in God as creator sit happily alongside theories like the Theory of Evolution?

● What are the advantages and disadvantages of classifying people by 'race'? The term 'ethnic' uses not only physical characteristics, but social and cultural information as well. Is it any better to use 'ethnic' information as a way of classifying people?

● Increasingly, as people move around the world, children are born to parents from different groups and grow up in very mixed societies. What do you think should be the future of terms like 'race' and 'ethnic' or any classification of people by physical appearance, culture or traditions?

Fig 15.10 Food gathering

● Do the Focus quotes lead you to believe that religion is a good way to combat victimisation of one group by another different group?

Find Out About

● The theory of evolution and how it explains humanity's divergence from the animals

● The ways in which Britain tries to prevent racial oppression or aggression among its citizens

● Evidence of oppression or aggression based on 'race' or 'ethnic' differences in the world today

● The part that religion seems to play in 'race' or 'ethnic' groupings of people

● Search the web under the heading **Race Relations**. Find out about organisations which are working in the field of race relations and what they do.

Homework

A Imagine you have to design a questionnaire which will provide the government with information on the 'ethnic' groups of people living in Britain. Would you include questions on people's faith or not? Explain your choice and why you made it.

or

B Try to write two simple laws which would prevent any one group victimising any other group in Britain on the grounds of physical difference or religious beliefs.

or

C You are a producer for Channel 4 TV and have been approached by a production company who want to make a documentary about tribes in Africa that still live in very simple ways. Write a 100-word memo setting out some guidelines which will ensure that the programme will not present the people of these tribes as inferior to the British audience who will see the programme.

Answers to page 61

Number 1: Vietnam
Number 2: America
Number 3: France
Number 4: Britain
Number 5: Britain

The Environment

Fig 16.1 Our responsibility?

The rights of nature

Does the environment have rights? What should those rights be and how should they be decided? Should it have rights of its own, or should these rights simply be a way of protecting our own species? The environment can't tell us what it wants or needs, but perhaps the signs are there if we know how to read them.

Fig 16.2 How nature responds to our abuses?

Crisis, what crisis?

Floods in Mozambique, avalanches in the Alps, freak fires in Australia . . . are these the results of changes to the environment brought about by human activity, or just regular natural events? There is little doubt that human actions have consequences; these actions might be too rapid and too widespread for nature to adapt quickly enough. For example, since the Industrial Revolution, we have been producing lots of pollution – particularly by burning fossil fuels like oil, coal and gas. This pollution is perfectly natural – it also comes out of volcanic eruptions – but so much has been released so quickly by human society that it might be causing environmental damage. However, pollution caused by human activity is often a side-effect of activities which have brought many benefits to human life – so should we just accept the environmental costs? Anyway, perhaps nature can cope perfectly well with our actions.

Causes and effects

- *Climate change* – the heating up of the Earth can cause climate change. This might result in more freak weather, as well as changes to when and how we grow crops. Also, sea-levels could rise. This could change the way humans live. It could also affect other living things. Acid rain, for example, destroys forests and everything which depends on them. The destruction of the ozone layer could mean that more UV radiation reaches Earth, with possible harmful effects for all life.

- *Pollution* – this is simple to cause and difficult to control. Sometimes it is dramatic – like the Exxon Valdez oil spill in Alaska. At other times it is slower and less obvious – like chemicals getting into water supplies by running off fields. Pollution can cause instant harm, like asthma from smog in cities. It can also harm more slowly, like the possible damaging effects of PCBs in our water supplies.

Fig 16.3 Oil spills – the effects can last for years

- *Running out of resources* – there might come a time when resources simply run out. Coal supplies in many areas are almost exhausted or too expensive to get at. David Bellamy says that if we increase our use of fossil fuels by 5%, they will all run out by 2047. Fish stocks are often controlled by quota schemes – fishermen are allowed to take only a certain amount each year. However, people have to make a living and if the amount of fish they are allowed to catch is cut, it could seriously harm their livelihood.

Fig 16.4 Nature pays for our jobs?

Competition

The human population is increasing quickly. We need more food, resources and room to live. Also, as the human species grows, pressure on other living things increases. For example, many species of animals are endangered or close to extinction because the places where they live have been over-used by humans. Also, in trying to meet our needs, many areas of the world have been used as sources for raw materials. Some of these are environmentally sensitive – like the Amazon rain forest.

Many environmentalists claim that we need to learn to use nature in a *sustainable* way. This means that we should be able to use what we have now in a way which means it will still be there in the future. This might mean reducing our needs for raw materials, or looking for alternatives. Some believe that in our competition with the rest of nature, we abuse our abilities and take unfair advantage.

DISCUSSION POINT

Do you think humans abuse nature? How? Why?

On the other hand

Perhaps we have a responsibility to our own species before other living things. Protecting the environment might be harmful for people. For example, in the developing world there is a need for more farmland. This might mean using up wild forest areas. What right does anyone have to deny developing world countries the benefits which these actions might bring? After all, the wealth of the developed world can often be traced to its use of nature for its own purposes. Also, if the use of chemical fertilisers produces cheaper food than can be achieved by growing it organically, what right do we have to force poor people to pay more, so that we can feel better about how we treat nature?

There's also the issue of jobs. Imagine a nuclear reprocessing plant is to be built in an area where there is high unemployment. Does anyone have the right to deny work to people locally because the work might be environmentally damaging?

DISCUSSION POINT

Should the needs of the environment come before the needs of people?

Fig 16.5 Wind farms – problem or solution?

Jews, **Christians** and **Muslims** all believe that nature is the gift of God and so is to be treated with care and respect. These faiths believe that mankind has been given special responsibility for looking after the Earth, which belongs to God. This is often called **stewardship**. The idea is that nature is to be respected because it belongs to God. Looking after it is a way of thanking God for the gift, as well as honouring his ownership of it.

> The world and all that is in it belongs to the Lord.

Psalm 24:1

> Then God said, 'and now we will make human beings; they will be like us and resemble us. They will have power over the fish, the birds, and all animals.'

Genesis 1:26

> The seventh year is to be a year of rest for the land ...

Leviticus 25:4

> He created man, giving him the ability to speak. The Sun and the Moon rotate in their orbits in an orderly way. The plants and trees bow down in adoration. He raised heaven on high and set the balance of all things so that mankind may not upset the balance. Keep the balance fairly and do not fall short in it.
>
> He laid out earth for his creatures, fruits and blossom-bearing palm, chaff-covered grain and scented herbs. Which of your Lord's blessings would you deny?

Surah 55:3–13

> He is the one who has spread out the earth and placed mountains and rivers on it, and has placed two pairs for every kind of fruit on it. He merges daylight into night.

Surah 13:2–3

In **Buddhism**, it is considered important to take only what is given to you. You should aim to show **loving kindness** to all living things. You should also try to avoid unnecessary harm where possible. Buddhists follow a middle path – neither too much nor too little of anything. Buddhists therefore should take what they need from nature and no more. They should also do this in a way which is kind and unharmful. Buddhists try to follow **five precepts**, or guidelines, for living. Two of these directly affect how we treat the natural world:

> I undertake to observe the rule to abstain from taking life; to abstain from taking what is not given.

In the Buddhist scriptures, the idea that you should take without harm is clear:

> As the bee takes the essence of a flower and flies away without destroying its beauty and perfume, so let the sage wander in this life.

Dhammapada 49

Sikhs believe that everything is a part of God and so should be given honour and respect just as God should.

> Air is the Guru, Water the Father, Earth the mighty Mother of all. Day and night are the caring guardians, fondly nurturing all creation.

Guru Granth Sahib

The Sikh should try to live his life in a spirit of **gratitude**. This will mean that he will show how grateful he is to God for all that he receives by his actions towards nature. Sikhs believe that God is the centre of the universe – behaving as if we are masters of nature means that we make ourselves Gods.

Hindus believe that the world is preserved and protected by **Vishnu**. Vishnu does this by coming to earth in living forms known as **Avatars**. Some of these are human and others not. This shows the Hindu that Brahman does not always think that humans are the only life-form with any value. Many Hindu festivals honour the non-human world, and gods in the form of animals are very popular.

Hindus believe that Brahman is in all things. Therefore all things deserve respect.

> I am the soul at the heart of all creatures.
>
> I am their origin, existence and decay.

Bhagavad-Gita 10:20

Activities

Text Questions

1 Why is deciding what rights the environment should have difficult?

2 How might human actions cause nature problems?

3 Why do some people think that humans have little effect on the environment?

4 What two effects could climate change have?

5 Name two forms of pollution.

6 What might increases in human population mean for other living things?

7 What alternative sources of energy could we use instead of fossil fuels?

8 How might fishing quotas harm people?

9 Should human needs come before the needs of the environment?

10 Why might a Christian or Jew think we should care for the environment?

11 What does Surah 55:3–13 say about why the environment is special?

12 Why might a Sikh believe in treating the environment carefully?

Discussion Points

● Who should decide what rights the environment should have? Governments? Individuals?

● Is there any evidence today of the effects of climate change?

● Is the impact of humans on nature too small to worry about?

● How much is pollution everyone's problem?

● Are fishing quotas necessary?

● Should some areas of the planet be left alone? Which? Why?

● Why might some religious people not be concerned about the environment?

● Should religious people become involved in environmental issues?

Find Out About

● Possible examples of the effects of climate change

● Global warming

● Ozone depletion

● Pollution

● The role played by religions in environmental pressure groups

● The views of representatives of faiths in your area on environmental issues, both local and global

● Search the web under the heading **Greenpeace**. Find out about the organisation's work.

Tasks

1 Design your own poster which illustrates the possible effects of environmental change. Entitle it: 'Environment in Crisis?' This should use images, as well as writing which explains possible causes and effects.

2 List possible environmental pollutants. State clearly where these are naturally produced or man-made. State also what possible damaging effects they could have.

3 Carry out the following role play:

You are the Managing Director of a company which wants to build a dam in an environmentally sensitive area. This dam will provide jobs, power and improvements in people's lives – in your opinion. It is backed by some of the local community, as well as the local and national government. However, environmentalists oppose it. You have come to address a public meeting on the issue.

Choose members of your class to play various characters at this meeting. You should be careful to ensure that some of the faith perspectives in the Focus section are represented.

4 Carry out a class debate: 'This house believes that the rights of humans come before the rights of nature.'

5 You are a Muslim. You have just joined Greenpeace. For some reason your parents are unhappy. Write a short note explaining your decision to them and showing how this fits with your Muslim faith.

6 Use the two Buddhist precepts on the previous page. Use these as the basis for an illustration, using images, poetry and writing.

Homework

A Find out about the organisation Greenpeace. Write a one-page article about it for an imaginary school magazine. Include its logo.

or

B Choose one of the specific environmental issues. Find out what a world faith has to say about it and write a short note about its views.

Animal Issues

Double standards?

In Britain, we like to think of ourselves as animal lovers. The amount of money spent worldwide on pet products is staggering. Most people would be angry if they found someone beating an animal in the street. When pets die, some people bury them in special pet cemeteries – spending a lot of money on their funerals.

On the other hand, while most people eat chicken, not many would want to eat dog. Also, when we are ill or want to make ourselves look better, we might use products which have been tested on animals. Even if we are meat eaters, could we kill the animal ourselves? Most of us visit zoos. Some people claim that these are just animal prisons. Where too, is our respect for animals when they are performing in the circus? What about horse-racing? Racing accidents have led many to argue that this popular sport is cruel. What also of fur-wearing? Recently a group of supermodels went naked to show their opposition to the wearing of furs.

What about genetically engineering animals for human body parts? Research into the growing of human hearts in genetically modified pigs has recently been banned – but because of how it might harm humans – not for the pigs' benefit. Also, have we the right to force dogs to act as police dogs, sniffer dogs, guide dogs for the blind?

Many people believe that in our treatment of animals we have double standards. We care deeply about the ones which are known to us, but not so much about others.

DISCUSSION POINT

Do you think we have double standards in our treatment of animals?

Fig 17.1 An anti-fur demonstration

What rights?

Many people believe that animals should have rights just like people. Sometimes they mean that animals should have exactly the same rights; other times that they should at least have the right to be treated fairly. Here are some of their reasons:

- How we treat animals says something about our own identity. A society can hardly be called just when it treats living things as if they don't matter.

- Why should one species (humans) have the right to treat other species badly? Isn't that just an abuse of our power?

- Animals can't communicate with us. So we need to look out for their interests.

- There is no need to treat animals badly. Human technology is now so advanced that most things we used to need animals for no longer apply.

- Most of the things we use animals for could be replaced with fairer alternatives, but we don't want to spend money doing this.

However, some people say that it makes no sense to give rights of any kind to animals.

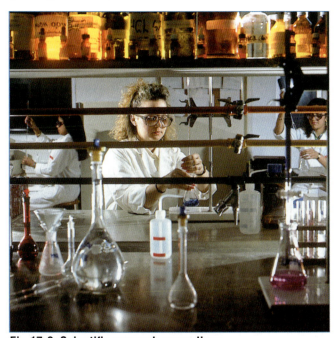

Fig 17.2 Scientific research saves lives

DISCUSSION POINT

What rights should animals have?
Why? How could these be brought
about?

It's always been that way

To change the way animals are treated, people would have to change many things about their lifestyle. Some would argue that this is wrong, because our relationship with animals has always been the way it is. It is natural for one species to use another for food and other benefits. Animals themselves kill and eat, and after all humans are just another form of animal. Nature is not gentle, it is cruel and violent – why should we expect humans to be any different?

Many of the improvements in our own lives have been brought about through the use of animals. For example, many life-saving drugs would never have existed if we hadn't been able to test them on animals first. Also, things like hunting are traditional activities and to ban them might destroy ways of life which have existed for a long time – and which sometimes are necessary for survival.

Besides, we now have the ability to use animals in ways which are much less cruel than they used to be. For example, slaughtering methods are now covered by strict laws to ensure that the animal doesn't suffer.

Sometimes there is just no alternative. The use of animals in medical research could produce great benefits (for humans *and* animals). What right does anyone have to deny these benefits to others? Humans and animals have always had an uneasy relationship – why should that change?

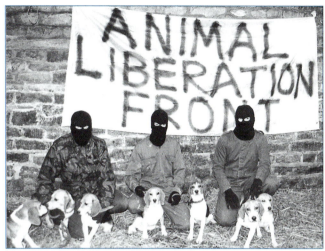

Fig 17.3 Animals – for human use?

Fighting back

If you believe that our current treatment of animals is not good and could be improved then what could you do?

- *Persuasion* – many groups carry out campaigns to make people more aware of animal rights issues.

- *Direct action* – some groups act directly against what they think is wrong. Some have carried out raids on animal experiment laboratories and freed captive animals. Hunt saboteurs try to get in the way of packs of hunting dogs.

- *Looking for alternatives* – some try to develop alternatives to animal products, and then try to persuade others to use them. The Body Shop for example, produces cosmetics which are cruelty-free.

DISCUSSION POINT

Do you think these forms of action are
equally acceptable?

Christians may have different views about animals. **Jesus** probably followed the **Jewish food laws**, and he did provide fish for others to eat (see Luke 5:1–11), so he probably wasn't a vegetarian. The first Christians followed the Jewish food laws too, though **Paul** soon taught that anything could be eaten:

> No food is of itself ritually unclean; but if a person believes that some food is unclean, it becomes unclean for him.

Romans 14:14

Paul was probably trying to make clear to the first Christians that they did not need to keep to the Jewish food laws. Later this idea was developed:

> Everything that God created is good, and nothing is to be rejected if it is received with thanksgiving.

Timothy 4:3–4

Many Christians believe that these were very specific answers to very specific problems at the time. They point to the Bible as something which stresses love and care for all living things, and that we should avoid taking life when it is not necessary. Such modern Christians might well argue that taking animal life today is not necessary in any form – and that to do so is an abuse of God's creation. This is all the more wrong because it is the abuse of the weak by the strong. The Bible teaches that it is a duty for the strong to help the weak.

Eastern faiths, like **Buddhism** and **Hinduism**, share the view that life should not be taken or harmed unnecessarily. Buddhist monks are forbidden to eat 10 kinds of meat. The principle of **ahimsa**, non-violence, also extends to animals. All living things are struggling towards release from the endless cycles of life, and how we behave in this life has consequences for the next. Unnecessary killing of, or cruelty to, animals will not help us towards a good **re-birth**.

> All things should be happy and at ease.

Metta Sutta

Buddhists believe that they should always be **mindful** of the needs of others, and this includes animals. However, Buddhists also follow the principle of **upaya kausala** (skilful means). The Buddha taught that you should judge each situation according to your own understanding of it and act as you think best. Thai Buddhist monks will accept meat if offered in their begging bowls. The eating of meat is normal for Buddhists in Tibet, where vegetables are difficult to grow.

Sikhs may eat meat provided that it is killed humanely. **Guru Nanak** taught that worrying too much about what you eat takes your mind off God. However, here too, there is a strong belief that God's creation should be cared for because it belongs to him.

> God's all-pervasive spirit indwells all the known and unknown creation.

Akal Murat

This means that disrespectful treatment of animals is in a sense disrespectful to God. **Namdhari Sikhs** however are strict vegetarians:

> Never eat meat.

Namdhari Rahit-nama

Muslims and **Jews** have strict food laws which describe clean and unclean foods. Foods should be prepared in a special way, and only certain foods may be eaten. Both, for example, do not eat pork.

> I find not in that which has been revealed to me anything forbidden to be eaten by one who wishes to eat it, unless it be an animal which has died itself, or blood from slaughtering or pork; for that surely is impure or unlawful meat ...

Surah 6:145

However, both Jews and Muslims believe that the food laws are not to be followed thoughtlessly. For example, when it is necessary to eat unclean foods to preserve life then that is permitted:

> But whoever is forced by necessity without wilful disobedience, nor transgressing due limits, certainly, your Lord is forgiving, most merciful.

Surah 6:145

Many **Humanists** are concerned about some of the problems associated with meat-eating. Humanists believe that we are the highest form of life in the Universe, but that doesn't give us the right to misuse our powerful position. Some Humanists have argued that meat-eating is wrong because:

- it is a wasteful process – it would be more environmentally friendly to eat only vegetable matter.
- it could have harmful effects on humans.
- it is the exploitation of the weak by the strong.
- it could lead to a careless attitude to life which might make cruelty to humans easier to take part in.

Activities

Text Questions

1 State two examples which show that the British might be thought of as animal lovers.

2 When might we use products which have been tested on animals?

3 Why might someone argue that we have double standards in the treatment of animals?

4 How might the treatment of animals affect our treatment of humans?

5 In what way is the inability of animals to communicate important in these issues?

6 How might someone argue that we don't need meat?

7 How has the use of animals helped humans?

8 Why do some people argue that hunting should not be banned?

9 How might people persuade others to treat animals more fairly?

10 What direct action has been carried out to support animal rights?

11 How might someone argue that Jesus wasn't a vegetarian?

12 How might a Christian argue for vegetarianism?

13 Should a Buddhist eat meat?

14 When might a Muslim ignore his food laws?

Discussion Points

- Do you think Britain is really a nation of animal lovers?
- Why are some people cruel to animals?
- What rights should animals have?
- Will people pay higher prices so that animals can be treated more fairly?
- Is tradition a good enough argument for continuing hunting?
- Does it matter how animals are treated?
- Do the strong have a duty to protect the weak?
- Does it matter what you do as long as your *intention* is right?

Find Out About

- Which animals are eaten around the world
- Experiments on animals for drugs and cosmetics – what is done, its supporters and opponents
- The work of animal rights organisations
- Pro and anti-hunting groups
- The actions of animal liberation groups
- The cruelty-free cosmetics industry
- Vegetarian groups within world faiths
- Search the web under the heading **Animal Rights**. Find out about the rights that different groups think animals should have.

Tasks

1 Design and carry out a survey in your school. Find out how many people have pets, how much they spend on them, what they have them for etc. Display your findings.

2 Choose one of the following topics and produce your own short project. You should include basic information, as well as arguments for and against the issue. Perhaps you could invite speakers to your school or make visits out of school. Topics: Meat-eating/Vegetarianism; Zoos; Animals in circuses; the use of animals in experiments. Once your project is completed, you should present your findings to the class in the form of a short talk.

3 Devise your own TV news item reporting on the issue of factory farming. This should be about 5 minutes or so in length. Perhaps your teacher could video your item and show it to the class.

4 Carry out a class debate: 'Testing drugs on animals is the best way to save human lives.'

5 Imagine you are an animal rights activist. You are in court charged with releasing animals from an experimental laboratory. Write and present the speech you would make in your defence. Someone in your class could then cross-examine you.

Homework

A Imagine that the government is about to decide whether horse-racing should be banned or not. There have been letters in the local paper supporting and opposing it. Write your own brief letter. You can choose whether to support or oppose the ban.

or

B Imagine you are a dog which has magically been given the power of speech! What might you say to humans about their treatment of animals generally? Write a short speech.

INDEX